H
R

HAMPSHIRE RAMBLES

Fifteen Country Walks around Hampshire

Nick Channer

———

With Historical Notes

COUNTRYSIDE BOOKS
NEWBURY, BERKSHIRE

First Published 1992
© Nick Channer 1992

COUNTRYSIDE BOOKS
3 Catherine Road
Newbury, Berkshire

ISBN 1 85306 171 9

Line illustrations by Phil Dollin
Sketch maps by Pip Challenger
Cover photograph of Watership Down
taken by Barry Shurlock

Produced through MRM Associates Ltd., Reading
Typeset by Paragon Typesetters, Sandycroft, Chester
Printed in England by J. W. Arrowsmith Ltd., Bristol

Acknowledgements

With grateful thanks to Sybil Tucker, David Jeffery, John Channer, Patrick Langdon and Antonio Zuccaro for their contribution to this book.

'They only know a country who are acquainted with its footpaths. By the roads, indeed, the outside may be seen; but the footpaths go through the heart of the land.'
Richard Jefferies

Contents

Area map showing locations of the walks.

Introduction

Hampshire's landscape is interesting and varied, from spectacular downland and the part of East Hampshire known affectionately as 'Little Switzerland' to salt marshes and fascinating coastal inlets. The jewel in Hampshire's crown is undoubtedly the New Forest, the largest remaining medieval forest in western Europe and a place of romance and beauty, but the county can also claim the 'Queen of the Chalk Streams', the delightful river Test which flows so peacefully through the lovely countryside. There is always something to interest the walker. The Iron Age hill fort of Danebury Ring, for example, or the house where the D-Day invasion was planned in 1944. Peaceful villages, restored canals, steam trains, country parks and trout streams are just some of the treats offered by the walks in this book.

The walks vary in length from 4 to 8 miles. Details are given about the location of each walk and for those who like to break their walk for refreshment the names of pubs providing meals and other places selling food on or near the route are mentioned.

The sketch map that accompanies each walk is designed to guide walkers to the starting point and give a simple but accurate idea of the route to be taken. For those who like the benefit of detailed maps the relevant Ordnance Survey series sheets 1:50,000 are recommended.

The historical notes at the end of each chapter are designed to provide basic information about the places of interest along the route.

No special equipment is needed to enjoy the countryside on foot, but do wear a stout pair of shoes and remember that at least one muddy patch is likely even on the sunniest day. Please remember the Country Code and make sure gates are not left open nor any farm animals are disturbed.

I hope you will gain as much enjoyment from these walks as I did in preparing them.

Nick Channer
March 1992

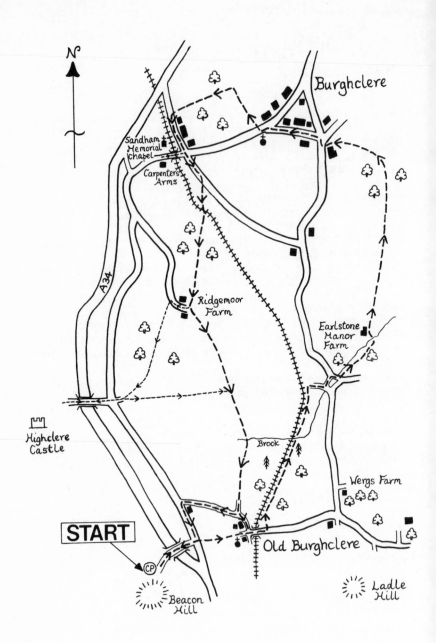

Beacon Hill
and Burghclere

Introduction: This is a walk combining fine downland views with sheltered tracks, green lanes and wooded paths, and includes a stretch along the route of a disused railway line. The walk begins at the foot of Beacon Hill, a much loved local beauty spot and landmark on the Hampshire/Berkshire borders. The hill rises to 858 ft and from the top you will gain a magnificent panoramic view of the Kennet Valley to the north and the Test Valley in the south.

From Beacon Hill the walk goes to Burghclere where a visit to the Sandham Memorial Chapel is a must. It was built in memory of H.W. Sandham and is famous for its superb murals by Stanley Spencer, immensely moving and probably his finest work.

The return route includes an optional diversion to Highclere Castle, the splendid country home of Lord Porchester. The house is open to the public at certain times during the summer months.

Distance: The main route is approximately 6 miles and will probably take about three hours to complete although this does not allow for time spent at the various places of interest including Sandham Memorial Chapel and Highclere Castle. Map: Ordnance Survey Landranger 174.

Refreshments: During the summer months an ice cream van is often to be seen in the car park at Beacon Hill. There is provision for picnicking too with tables and benches etc. The Carpenter's Arms in Burghclere is an ideal place to take a break being midway along the route. The pub has a range of bar food and a restaurant. The Carnarvon Arms on the spur to Highclere Castle also provides bar meals.

How to get there: From south or mid Hampshire proceed along the A34 and north of the exit for Whitchurch look for the sign to Beacon Hill. The free car park lies just to the west of the main road.

The Walk: If time permits a climb to the summit of Beacon Hill is worthwhile. For obvious reasons it is probably easier to attempt the steep ascent before you start the actual walk rather than afterwards!

At the top of the hill you are at once in a tranquil world of attractive colours and splendid views. Beacon Hill is the final resting place of the fifth Earl of Carnarvon and his grave is on the western slopes. If you look to the north you will glimpse the magnificent architecture of Highclere Castle beyond the many trees. Away to the east is Ladle Hill, an Iron Age hill fort.

Retracing your steps to the car park should be an easier process and once there follow the road up to the road bridge over the A34. Cross the bridge and when you reach the T junction go left for a few yards and then over the road to a waymarked footpath. Take the path and descend the bank between wire fences. Pass through the gate and walk along the field boundary noting the fine downland view on the right. Ahead a church tower peeps into view through the trees.

In the field corner continue ahead onto a grassy path drawing level with All Saints' church, Old Burghclere. Go through a white gate onto a gravelled drive, passing the buildings of Burghclere Manor on your right. Soon you reach the road and, disregarding the turning on the right and the road on the left, proceed straight ahead, signposted Kingsclere. After a few steps you cross over a bridge and then immediately beyond it bear left onto a footpath. Away to the extreme right are the slopes of Watership Down, the setting for Richard Adams' legendary story of rabbits.

Keep to the path running alongside the trees and hedgerow and shortly before you reach the field corner pass through the wide gap in the hedge onto the old railway line. This line used to run from Didcot to Southampton and was closed in the Beeching era after nearly 80 years in continuous service. Turn right and walk along the route of the old line heading in a northerly direction. The enclosed path is particularly attractive in places where it runs alongside bursts of fir trees and peaceful glades below the embankment.

Further on, the views are unrestricted as you look back towards the distinctive outline of Beacon Hill on the southern horizon. Glancing to the right as you head along the old track, a TV mast is visible in the far distance high in the hills. Virtually wherever you look the scenery is delightful.

When, eventually, you reach the old railway arch leave the former line by either bank, though the left hand exit is easier to negotiate and less steep. At the top turn right and follow the track down to the road. Again, the downland views are impressive. At the road bear left and then after a few yards, at the junction, swing right. After a few moments you reach a path on the left running through the trees.

Follow the path and after some time when you reach a stony track turn left towards a large red brick house and its farm buildings (Earlstone Manor Farm). Pass over the brook with its waters chattering noisily below you and veer right before the entrance to the house and the buildings. The track then bears left and soon passes the entrance to a pair of red brick farmworkers' cottages. Continue along this track as it cuts its way through some exceptionally attractive country. There are several curves in the path as the woodland becomes more dense.

The track then bends sharp left. Soon the woodland is replaced by hedgerow and fields and away to the left on the horizon is the tip of Beacon Hill. Before long the track reaches the road. Turn right into Well Street and immediately left at the junction. You are now in the village of Burghclere and heading along Church Lane. You soon come to a T junction at which stands a war memorial. The church is to the left on this corner.

Bear left for a few yards and then cross the road to a waymarked path. Follow the path between trees and hedgerow. Soon there are glimpses of houses on the left across the field. On reaching a stile cross over into the field and continue ahead along the boundary, keeping to a grassy path. At the next stile cross out onto a stony track and turn left. The track cuts between a line of trees on the right and a hedgerow on the left. Further on, the track becomes a tarmac drive serving various private houses and bungalows.

Proceed along the drive through the avenue of trees and on reaching the junction swing left onto a road running alongside a row of houses with the route of the old railway line on the right down amongst the trees. Follow the road along the embankment until you arrive at a junction. Turn right and cross the bridge over the defunct line. Just beyond it on the right is the entrance to Sandham Memorial Chapel. The Carpenter's Arms is a few yards further along the road on the left.

Retrace your steps to the railway bridge and then bear right down Spring Lane. Walk down the lane. The first house on the right was originally Highclere railway station. Rather confusingly, the station at Old Burghclere was called Burghclere so Highclere was chosen as the name for this station!

Follow the road with good view ahead towards Watership Down and Hannington on the skyline. Pass a cottage on the left and continue. Ignore a footpath on the right running between fences and carry on for a short distance until you reach two farm gates either side of the lane. Turn right over the stile into the field and then go diagonally left towards the corner. Look to the right as you cross the field for a good view of the long-disused signal box at Highclere station.

Aim now for a path hidden among the trees identified by a footbridge over the ditch followed by a stile. Take the path up the old railway embankment. At the top cross the route of the old track and then take the path down the other bank. At the bottom proceed over the footbridge and the stile and then veer left into a field enclosed by trees. Proceed ahead across the field, which can be very boggy in wet weather, and aim for the wide gap in the trees (not to be confused with the gap in the right hand corner of the field).

Go through the gap into the adjacent field and continue ahead along the field edge with a belt of light woodland on the right.

Follow the field border curving to the right and very soon the buildings of Ridgemoor Farm come into view. On reaching the end of the woodland head out across the open field towards the farm. Pass a pond just before the boundary and then join a track at the farm where the route of the walk meets the start of the diversion to Highclere Castle (see below).

To continue the *main walk* turn left and follow the track away from Ridgemoor Farm. In a while the track begins a gradual climb and soon passes a cross track. Continue up the slope and as you descend the other side pause for a moment to admire the rich spread of countryside below you. Avoid the turning on the right and keep ahead until you reach the road after about ½ mile.

You are now back at Old Burghclere and may make a choice at this point for the last stage of the walk. If you turn right you will soon reach the road junction where you turn left and then right over the A34 to reach the car park at Beacon Hill. Alternatively, to avoid any road walking, continue ahead and return to Beacon Hill via Burghclere Manor and All Saints' church. The entrance to the former will appear shortly on the right.

The spur to Highclere Castle: On reaching Ridgemoor Farm turn right and after several minutes when the drive swings right, bear left onto a waymarked track. Follow it up the slope through an enclosed tunnel of trees bordered by high banks and farmland. The track soon narrows to a path climbing steadily through the hills. At length you reach a track and over to the left at this point are glorious far reaching views across a wide wooded landscape stretching well beyond the Hampshire/Berkshire boundary. The outskirts of Newbury are clearly visible and to the right of them the distinctive outline of Greenham Common Airbase.

Turn right and follow the track heading towards Highclere Castle. There are very good views on the left of nearby Beacon Hill. Soon the track becomes a metalled road and on the right there are various buildings and timber barns. When you reach the road junction in a couple of minutes or so go straight across (The Carnarvon Arms is a few hundred yards along the road to the right) following the sign for Highclere Castle. Proceed across the bridge over the A34 and into the grounds of the castle.

Keep on the drive through the trees following the signs for Highclere Castle until you reach the house, set in glorious parkland in the North Hampshire hills. On leaving Highclere retrace your steps to the bridge over the A34. Proceed to the junction and continue ahead along the narrow lane opposite. Follow the lane between trees, thick hedgerows and bushes. On reaching the wooded path traversed on the outward leg of this spur continue past it keeping to the track, with splendid views of West Berkshire providing the northern backdrop on this stretch.

Proceed ahead between high hedgerows and trees and soon the track drops down to a major junction, at which point you rejoin the main route of the walk. Turn right here and follow the track to Old Burghclere. At the road either turn right, left at the road junction and then first right over the A34 to Beacon Hill, or continue ahead to Burghclere Manor and retrace your steps to the car park passing All Saints' church on the left.

Historical Notes

Beacon Hill: On these grassy slopes some of the earliest experimental aeroplane flights were made by pioneer aviator Geoffrey de Havilland and his brother Frank in 1909.

Beacon Hill is an Iron Age hill fort defended by a ditch, bank and counterscarp bank. Its single entrance faces the natural approach along a ridge and is protected by extra banks. The sites of about 20 round huts can be traced within the defences.

The fifth Earl of Carnarvon expressed a desire to be buried up here overlooking his home Highclere Castle, where he was born on 26th June 1866. He became interested in archaeology when at Cambridge and for 16 years he and Howard Carter conducted field work and excavations in Egypt. Their most famous discovery came in November 1922 — Tutankhamun's tomb.

Sandham Memorial Chapel: The chapel was built in 1926-27 by Mr and Mrs J.L. Behrend who commissioned it as a war memorial and a specific monument to H.W. Sandham, who died in 1919 from an illness contracted during the First World War in Macedonia (now part of Yugoslavia). The architect was Lionel Pearson and Stanley Spencer was responsible for the hugely impressive and ambitious murals. They took six years to finish and are reputed to be the most important series of decorative paintings produced in England this century, representing scenes from the Great War in which Spencer served as an orderly in a military hospital. The National Trust-owned chapel, which is flanked by two almshouses, is open between April and the end of October Wednesday to Sunday (including Good Friday) 11.30 am—6 pm; November until the end of March Saturday and Sunday only 11.30 am—4 pm; closed Christmas Day and 1st January.

Highclere Castle occupies the site of the summer palace of the Bishops of Winchester. Henry Herbert, who became Earl of Carnarvon in 1793, employed 'Capability' Brown to create the particularly beautiful park circa 1775. The present house was constructed from the designs of Sir Charles Barry (the architect of the Houses of Parliament) between 1839-42 in a Renaissance style. The house is open Wednesday—Sunday inclusive from the end of June until the end of September, 2 pm—6 pm, last admission 5 pm.

'The Hampshire Highlands': Linkenholt and The Test Way

Introduction: The aptly-named 'Hampshire Highlands' are probably more commonly known as the North Hampshire Downs, a stretch of high downland country in the top north west corner of the county. Here and there peaceful little villages lie undisturbed in the hills; isolated communities that, thankfully and perhaps not surprisingly, have changed little over the centuries.

The walk makes for the point where three counties meet in remote, hidden country amid hills and woods. From here it follows a lengthy section of the beautiful Test Way, one of Hampshire's long distance footpaths, as far as the hamlet of Netherton. A gentle pull through the fields then brings you to the pretty hill-top village of Linkenholt with spectacular views across the rolling 'highlands'.

Distance: The walk is about 4½ miles and should take about two hours. Map: Ordnance Survey Landranger 174.

Refreshments: Apart from The Boot at Linkenholt there are no pubs on the route. The Boot provides real ale served from the cask and a good menu including ploughman's, home-made soup and basket meals.

How to get there: From the A343 Andover-Newbury road at Hurstbourne Tarrant follow the signs for Ibthorpe and Upton. At Upton continue north to Vernham Street and The Boot is about ½ mile to the north of the village at Littledown, just to the west of Linkenholt.

The Walk: From the car park at The Boot go out to the road, bear left and then, almost immediately, turn right at the junction, following the lane between hedgerows.

Keep on this quiet country road for some time and after a little more than ½ mile, as you approach a sharp left hand bend, take a waymarked track on the right running between bushes and trees and banks of undergrowth. Further

17

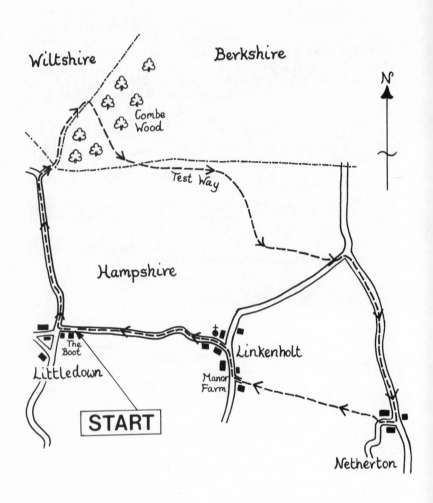

up the track, just before the field at the top, is the point at which three counties meet – Hampshire, Berkshire and Wiltshire.

As you come up towards the field bear left into the adjacent field and follow the right hand boundary, keeping the hedge and trees hard on your right. In the corner continue onto a grassy path with trees on the right and a plantation on the left. On reaching a footpath sign with arrows pointing in both directions proceed into the woods, following the county boundary between Wiltshire on the left and Berkshire on the right. Keep on the path down through cool, shaded woods, dense in places, until at last it emerges from the trees to provide glorious views of Hampshire downland with the Test Way a little further down at the bottom. On reaching the track, with Sheepless Hill in front of you, turn right and follow the Test Way; you are now entering Berkshire.

The Test Way is a long distance footpath of some 44 miles providing walkers with the opportunity to explore this famous chalk stream as it meanders delightfully through the Hampshire landscape. Beginning at Totton on the outskirts of Southampton and finishing at Inkpen Beacon on the Hampshire/Berkshire border, the route was devised by Hampshire County Council.

Stay on the Test Way for a while as it cuts through Combe Wood and the sheltered folds and desolate valleys of the 'Hampshire Highlands'. Avoid a track on the left and continue. After about ¼ mile cross the county boundary back into Hampshire. Follow the track, avoiding all turnings and at length you will arrive at the road.

Bear left and at the junction take the road to the right signposted Netherton and Hurstbourne Tarrant. Follow the lane between fields and hedgerows. On reaching Netherton turn right at the footpath sign, opposite a wooden fence, and proceed along the gravelled drive with a large barn and a thatched cottage on the right.

Further up, a lychgate leads into a quiet graveyard though there is no longer a church here. Nowadays the hamlet of Netherton is served by the church of St Barnabas at nearby Faccombe. Only the gravestones remain, nestling peacefully among the trees. On leaving the graveyard swing left, pass a thatched cottage and then take the footpath on the left.

Cross the field by going diagonally right and in the far corner there is a stile amid the trees and undergrowth. Go over it and follow the path round to the left through the foliage. Negotiate the next stile and then one more. In the next field proceed ahead by keeping hard to the right hand boundary. Cross the fence and follow the waymarked track heading towards some farm buildings. Pass to the right of the buildings and on reaching the road turn right and head down the lane. Note the entrance to the farm on the left and just beyond it the interestingly-named Jesse Dewey Cottage. Beyond the cottage bear left in the centre of Linkenholt, signposted Vernham Street. Pass the village post office and continue with the church on the right. Follow the road through the village and out between fields; here there are lovely far reaching views across the 'Hampshire Highlands'.

The Boot car park where the walk began will be found on the left about ¾ mile from the centre of Linkenholt.

Historical Notes

The Boot: This locally-famous brick and flint inn was built during the 15th century. Originally, there was a cobbler on this site — hence the pub's name. Note the boot swinging from the pub sign out by the road!

Linkenholt: The village includes some attractive period property. The church has a Norman doorway and in the stonework adorning two windows are fossilized sea-urchins or 'shepherds' crowns'.

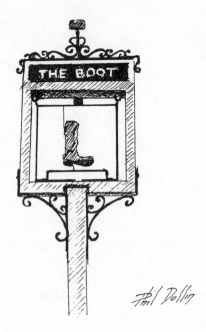

The River Test at Whitchurch and Laverstoke

Introduction: This fascinating ramble takes you through the pretty Test Valley, beginning in the old coaching town of Whitchurch where a silk mill, open to the public, straddles Britain's purest trout stream.

It is always interesting to read of a man who, through his own determination, built a business empire, particularly one which has been successful for over 200 years. Henry Portal came to Britain from France as a refugee at the end of the 17th century and established a paper mill providing paper for the Bank of England notes. The route of this walk takes you past the little mill where he modestly began his business, and then on to the estate village of Laverstoke which became the permanent home of Portal's expanded industry.

Distance: The walk is about 5½ miles in length. It should take two to two and a half hours to complete but allow a little longer if you intend to look round Whitchurch and perhaps visit the silk mill. Map: Ordnance Survey Landranger 185.

Refreshments: There are a number of inns serving good food and drink in Whitchurch including The King's Arms and The Bell. The Watership Down Inn approximately halfway round the circuit provides bar meals.

How to get there: Whitchurch is about 6 miles to the east of Andover, just off the main A34. There is free parking in the town; the free car park in Test Road, just off the Winchester Road, is suggested for this walk.

The Walk: From the car park in Test Road walk along to the Winchester Road junction and turn left. Pass Whitchurch silk mill on the right, cross over the river Test and after the tree-shaded driveway to a large house on the left, take a footpath running between brick walls also on the left. After a short distance pass through a kissing gate and continue ahead. At the end of the path turn left into McFauld Way. When the road swings right after a few yards proceed along

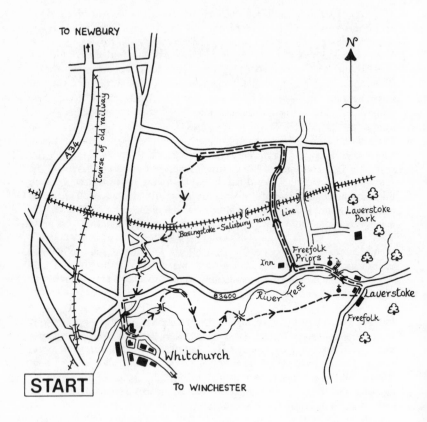

the footpath and follow it as it skirts school playing fields. Very soon the path joins the river Test on your left.

Shortly, with the grounds of the school still on your right, you reach a sharp left hand bend. Take the bend and cross the river by a footbridge. On your left now is the attractive Town Mill poised above the swirling waters of the Test. This is one of a number of mills encountered on this walk. At the end of the bridge turn right and follow a path beside a wooden panel fence. All around you is a network of delightful streams and pretty river backwaters.

Cross a wooden footbridge followed by another smaller bridge and then walk along a path. When you reach the end of the path do not walk ahead up the hill to the main road but turn right and proceed along a lane between rows of modern bungalows. Soon the dwellings peter out and now the lane becomes a rough track bordered by fields and watercress beds. Continue ahead onto a grassy path keeping the hedgerow on your left. When you reach a gap in the hedge go through it and maintain the same direction with the hedgerow now on your right.

Shortly the river Test appears again on your right and then very soon you reach the field corner. Follow the path round to the left and after a few steps there is a stile beneath some trees. Pass over the stile, turn left and keep to the perimeter of the field, with delightful views of Bere Mill over on the right nestling peacefully in the valley. When you reach a narrow lane turn right and walk along it. After a few minutes you pass over the river once again − this time by means of a very elegant brick built bridge which is worth pausing to admire, as is the charmingly preserved Bere Mill away on the right.

Walk past the entrance to the mill and you may spot the odd trout or two on the shallow river bed. At the end of the lane cross a stile in front of you with two cottages on your left. Proceed ahead up the grassy track for some time towards a distant line of oaks. On reaching them bear left and walk alongside them for a few paces and then follow the path round to the right. At this point you have a delightful view of the Test pottering through the tranquil valley below. The spire of St Mary the Virgin at Laverstoke watches over it from the tree-covered slopes on the north bank.

When you reach a wooden section of fencing in the far boundary of the field, cross it and walk ahead towards a hedgerow and two cottages. Pass through an opening in the hedge and then turn left and walk along the lane towards the little church. Turn right before reaching it, into the churchyard. This is St Nicholas' at Freefolk. No longer required for worship, the church is maintained by the Redundant Churches fund. There is a notice on the door advising you where to locate the key if you wish to see inside it. The church is shared by the villagers of both Laverstoke and Freefolk.

Leave the churchyard by the same gate. Turn left and after a few steps you reach a stile. Pass over the stile and walk along the field. Note a very attractive house set in delightful gardens on your left. In the left hand corner of the field cross over a stile with the Test on your left and proceed ahead. There is a playing field on your right now and the Sports and Social Club is ahead of you on the right. Make for a flight of steps leading you up the bank to the right of a building. At the top of the bank walk towards the road with the club car park on your right.

On reaching the road turn left and head down to the junction. Opposite you now are the buildings and main entrance of Laverstoke Mill. Turn left at the junction and walk along the road. Just beyond a garage the stretch of pavement ends so for safety cross the road and keep to the pavement on the other side. Away on your right can be seen Laverstoke Park, famous for its beeches. Laverstoke House, 18th century home of the Portals, is not visible from the road.

Pass into Freefolk, cross the river Test again and then note the entrance to Laverstoke Park on the right. There is a quaint little lodge here on the left hand side of the drive. Just beyond the entrance is a narrow lane with a public footpath sign on the right, immediately before a row of striking thatched cottages built surprisingly just before the Second World War for employees of the paper mill. Take the turning and walk up the lane to the church of St Mary the Virgin. After a visit to the church return to the lane and head back to the main road past the old village primary school on the left. Much of the building round here including the school is the work of the Portal family.

At the road junction turn right and continue through the village of Laverstoke, passing the estate workers' cottages on the right. Bear right, further on, signposted 'The Watership Down Inn' and pass the pub on the left. Watership Down itself is a few miles to the north on the Hampshire/Berkshire border but this part of the Test Valley features in Richard Adams' famous rabbit tale.

Follow the narrow lane, which provides good views over the surrounding countryside. Cross over the Basingstoke-Salisbury railway line and progress along the lane. At the triangular junction bear left and keep to the road, with pleasant pastoral views. Pass a drive on the right to Wooldings Farm and at the bottom of the hill; avoiding a turning on the left, just as the road begins to climb again there is a footpath sign and a gap in the hedge on the left. Pass into the field and walk along its left boundary, all the time keeping close to the hedgerow on your immediate left. In the corner follow the path round to the right and climb up the hillside with the railway embankment on your left.

At the top of the hill turn left and pass through the railway arch. Just beyond it bear right through a gate into a field and then go diagonally across it to the top left corner. Here, between the hedge on your left and the garden of a semi-detached house on your right, is a stile taking you out into the road. Walk ahead along the road passing Whitchurch police station on your left. At the junction just beyond it turn left into Lynch Hill Park and proceed along the road between the houses. When it becomes flanked by bungalows watch for a footpath running alongside the garden of the third bungalow on the right (number 37). Follow the path down beside some trees and gardens to join the road at the end of a cul-de-sac. Cross over and join another path running between houses.

Descend quite steeply now and after a few yards you reach a junction of paths beside a street lamp. Turn right and follow the path through the trees with excellent views of Whitchurch below you. When the path forks, bear left and continue between pretty cottages and colour-washed villas. Gradually you descend to the road. Turn right and walk into the centre of Whitchurch. At the main junction swing left into Winchester Road and the car park in Test Road will be found after a short distance.

Historical Notes

Whitchurch Silk Mill: Restored by the Hampshire Buildings Preservation Trust, the mill is situated on Frog Island on the Test. The mill building had a clock installed in 1812 to celebrate the victory at Waterloo as well as a distinctive cupola. The mill you see today was built about 1800 and the product created here was shalloon, a type of worsted with origins in Chalons in France. By the beginning of the 20th century the mill was manufacturing silk rather than wool. Then, in the 1930s, the lovely old water wheel became redundant as the source of power altered to electricity. The delicate material handstitched at Whitchurch often ends up being worn in court by Britain's top barristers, hence the phrase 'taking silk'. University dons have been known to wear Whitchurch silk and the mill also supplies the silk for dinner jacket lapels and much more besides.

The silk mill is open all year Tuesday – Sunday 10.30 am – 5 pm.

Bere Mill: This is where Henry Portal operated his paper-making business before moving to larger premises at Laverstoke. No longer in commercial use, the mill has been carefully preserved through the years and today remains a charming old building in a delightful setting, little changed since the period when it was occupied by Portal.

Laverstoke Mill: The founder of the mill, Henry Portal, came from France. He was born Henri de Portal into a Huguenot family. When he was still a boy his family's chateau was invaded by the soldiers of Louis XIV during the persecution of the Huguenots following the revocation of the Edict of Nantes in 1685. Young Henri escaped death by hiding in an oven while the chateau was searched. The boy fled across the Channel to England and became an apprentice at a paper mill at South Stoneham on the Itchen. He worked there alongside other Huguenot refugees. Sir William Heathcote, squire of Hursley, whom he met at South Stoneham gave him the opportunity to begin his own business. Through his patron's uncle Sir Gilbert Heathcote, Governor of the Bank of England, he gained the contract to produce the paper used for the Bank of England notes — an order that has lasted to this day.

Whitchurch: Before the bypass the town was a bustling junction of several major roads. It was at its most important during the coaching era with passengers stopping to change from one long distance coach to another and often staying at The White Hart Hotel. Charles Kingsley came here on occasions and was inspired to write of his visits to the town.

The parish church of All Hallows on the west side of the town has some interesting features. There is an Anglo-Saxon memorial stone in the church to a woman who it is believed was a nun from nearby Wherwell Priory. The Latin inscription reads: 'Here lies the body of Frithburga, buried in peace'. For many years bellringers at the church used the stone to stand on.

The former Master of the Rolls, Lord Denning, was born over his parents' draper's shop beside the town hall in 1899.

Wherwell and Harewood Forest

Introduction: Wherwell, which sprawls along the western banks of the Test, is surely everybody's idea of a charming English village. Like its near neighbours Longparish and St Mary Bourne it is considered one of the prettiest villages in North Hampshire. But the calm, parochial scene belies a wealth of history and legend that surrounds the place. The same can be said of nearby Harewood Forest through which the walk passes. A thousand years ago it was the setting for a machiavellian scheme of murder by royal command. The walk also follows a stretch of the Test Way.

Distance: This walk is about 6 miles in length. Allow about three hours to complete it. Map: Ordnance Survey Landranger 185.

Refreshments: There are two excellent public houses on the route: The Royal Oak at Goodworth Clatford and The White Lion at Wherwell, both of which serve food.

How to get there: Goodworth Clatford is about 2 miles south of Andover just off the main A3057. It is well signposted and there is permitted parking in the car park of The Royal Oak.

The Walk: From the car park turn left and then left again. After a few yards there is a delightful river scene on your right. This is the river Anton — a tributary of the Test. Pass over the river and after a few yards the road bends round to the left. As it does so leave its smooth metalled surface and walk ahead onto a path. Immediately you are faced with a choice of two paths. Take the one on the right and follow it with a fence and hedgerow on your left and fields either side.

Because of the nearby river the land here is very low lying and can often be rather wet and muddy. Soon the path becomes more enclosed with a steep bank on your left and trees and undergrowth on the right. Very shortly you are joined by the river meandering alongside. Keep to the path with the Anton on your right and soon the countryside opens out again as you skirt the right hand edge

27

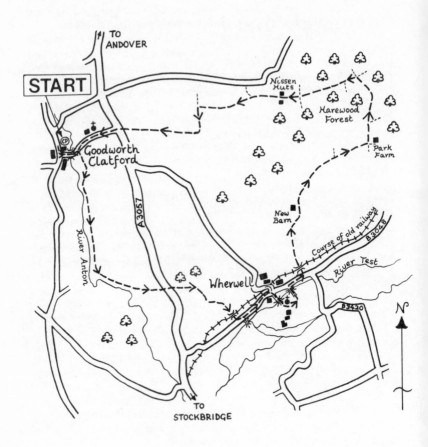

of a field. After a few moments, with the river now a short distance away from you, pass to the right of the Fullerton Water Pollution Control Works. Continue ahead along the right hand boundary of a field. Keep on the path as it heads for the field corner and proceed into the trees and then into the next field by means of a gate. Skirt the field by its right hand edge and after some time you reach the road. Cross it and pass through a gate immediately opposite.

Walk up the hill by way of a clear, well-defined path cutting between the bushes and scrub. When you reach the footpath sign at the top, pause and glance back for a stunning view of the soft Hampshire countryside beneath you. You can glimpse the river winding lazily through the trees on its way south. Proceed across the grass with fencing either side of you and make for a wooden gate ahead. When you reach the gate pass through it and continue along a narrow path. After a short distance the path leaves the field edge and runs between hedgerows. Continue along the well-defined path.

When you reach the end of the avenue of trees you find yourself on a high somewhat windy and exposed plateau with spectacular views to the south. Turn left here and walk down the slope keeping to the right hand edge of the field. Follow the track round to the right and walk along the right hand boundary of the field. After a few moments, as you approach the trees the path curves to the left and then passes beneath the disused railway bridge barely visible amidst the spread of trees and growth. A few steps beyond the bridge you reach the road. Turn left towards the village of Wherwell but leave the road after a few yards by turning right along a footpath which almost at once takes you over the river Test by means of a long wooden bridge. This is a particularly scenic stretch of the river with the water edging its way round a crop of wooded islands in midstream. The river divides nearby and the tributary heading away to the east is the river Dever, or Bullington Stream as it is otherwise known.

Return now to the road. Go right, and soon you reach the delightful village centre of Wherwell at a junction beside The White Lion public house, a former coaching inn, parts of which date back to the 17th century. Turn left and walk up the road for a few yards until, after the bend, you reach an old railway bridge. This is another slight deviation from the main route of the walk but it is worth making in order to gaze from the bridge at the site of the old station below you. What was the station building is now home to some of the villagers and nearby the gardens of some modern bungalows have replaced the old railway line. Gazing at such a peaceful domestic scene it is hard to visualise the steam and engine noise of past years.

Now retrace your steps to the junction but instead of continuing along the main street of the village or turning right and heading in the direction from which you have recently come, walk straight ahead onto a narrow lane between houses. After crossing the Test watch for a path that leads you into the churchyard. Take the path to visit the church of St Peter and Holy Cross.

As you leave it turn left and immediately pass a gate into the grounds of Wherwell Priory on your right. Make for the lych gate below the trees and then walk back towards the village along a lane with some very attractive thatched cottages. Before you reach the main street pass over the Test once again, as it leaps noisily between the houses. When you arrive at the junction with the war memorial in front of you turn right and walk along the road for a short distance.

Very shortly, just beyond a row of thatched cottages, is a stony track on the left which passes beneath the former railway line. Take the track and follow it for some time as it cuts between fields, coinciding now with the route of the Test Way. In a while you reach some farm buildings together with an attractive white cottage. Follow the track to the right of them and keep to it as again it cuts through the fields, twisting, turning and unravelling itself before you. As it hugs an area of extensive woodland on your left you soon approach some old buildings.

Turn left immediately before a corrugated shed. Walk away from the buildings and downhill into woodland. At the bottom of the hill follow the track as it swings sharply to the right. At the junction, after a few steps proceed straight across ignoring paths left and right. The left hand path as you will see is marked 'private'. Walk along a concrete track for some time and at the next fork keep left. You are now deep in the southern section of Harewood Forest, the northern half being to the other side of the main A303. This area of ancient sprawling forest offers the walker a considerable measure of peace and beauty. If you are lucky you may spot some of the forest's fallow deer skipping gracefully through the trees. Keep on the path for about ½ mile and then when you reach the junction turn left and walk along a similar, very straight track cutting through the trees. Avoid turnings to the left and right, pass over a cross track, and then walk between two wartime Nissen huts. Continue along the track through the trees.

After a few yards it veers to the left but the route of the walk continues ahead beneath the trees that here form a kind of tunnel. Descend the slope and walk up the other side.

Follow the path through the gate into the field. Turn left and walk along the perimeter following the arrows. When you reach a wide gap in the left hand boundary marked with an arrow pass through the gap into the next field. After a minute or two pass through another wide gap into the field on the left and then follow the right hand edge of the field. A row of pylons can be seen ahead with good views across to Goodworth Clatford. At the bottom of the field in the corner cross the stile bear left and then take the next track on the right down to the road. When you reach it after about five minutes take the road opposite (signposted Goodworth Clatford). Pass the church on the right and near it an interesting towered timber building in the middle of a field. The road cuts between various cottages, houses and bungalows. Pass over the river Anton once again and after a few steps you reach the junction with the main street and The Royal Oak on the right where the walk started.

Historical Notes

The railway line at Wherwell: The railway connecting the London-Salisbury line with the Andover-Southampton line carried passenger trains until 1931 and freight until 1956. It was opened in 1885, having been built by the London and South Western in order to prevent the rival Great Western Company from providing a through train service from Paddington to Bournemouth. For some reason it became known as 'The Nile' and was particularly appreciated by Queen Victoria who was said to have specifically requested that Royal Trains use this route when she travelled to Osborne House on the Isle of Wight. The track featured in the original film version of 'The Ghost Train' made in the 1920s. During the Second World War trains carried ammunition along the line to Harewood Forest where it was stored.

Wherwell: There are many legends surrounding Wherwell but perhaps the most interesting and imaginative is the one concerning the cockatrice. There are a number of versions of this tale but the following one, from 'Wherwell − An Anthology' is probably the most absorbing: 'A duck laid an egg in the crypt of the abbey which was hatched by a toad and turned into a cockatrice − a kind of dragon. It grew to an enormous size and had an insatiable appetite. It flew from the abbey in search of food and many of the villagers were snatched and taken to the abbey lair to be eaten. This state of affairs could not continue and a reward of four acres of land was offered to anyone who would kill the cockatrice. A man named Green polished a piece of steel until it gleamed like a mirror and lowered it down to the beast's lair. On seeing its reflection the cockatrice fought until it was exhausted and then Green ran the beast through with a javelin and claimed his reward. Today in Harewood Forest there is still an area known as Green's Acres'.

Wherwell Priory: The nunnery may well have been founded in AD 986 for the least expected reasons. It is thought that the Saxon Queen Elfrida established it as an act of repentance following several dark deeds for which she had been responsible some years earlier.

Eager to meet Elfrida, daughter of a duke and a renowned beauty, and considering her as a possible marriage partner, King Edgar had despatched one of his courtiers Earl Aetholwold to look her over and report back. Unfortunately for the king, his earl was totally taken by the charm and beauty of the girl and he promptly married her himself. Suspecting something of the sort might have taken place, Edgar personally visited Elfrida at Wherwell.

On discovering the truth about her new husband's mission and realising she had missed the chance of becoming queen, Elfrida turned her remarkable charms fully towards King Edgar. Together the couple plotted to kill Aetholwold. Edgar arranged for a hunting trip for the two of them in Harewood Forest. There in AD 965 the Saxon king stabbed him to death, thus enabling Elfrida to marry him. When he died, Edgar was succeeded to the throne by his eldest son Edward who was the queen's stepson. However Elfrida was anxious to see her own son Ethelred (the Unready) become king and the dark streak in her appeared once more. She had Edward stabbed to death at Corfe Castle in AD 978. Her own son then succeeded to the throne. Elfrida was linked with several other murders, but after founding Wherwell priory she lived a life of seclusion and simplicity there, no doubt haunted by her own conscience. She died in 1002. The priory prospered under a number of good abbesses, perhaps the most notable being Euphemia — a medieval Florence Nightingale who was responsible for many improvements to the large estates which included among others the manors of Wherwell, Goodworth and Longparish.

Harewood Forest: North of the A303 is 'Dead Man's Plack', a tall monument erected in 1862 recalling the murder of Earl Aetholwold by King Edgar in the forest in AD 965. The forest was once much larger. It is not on the same scale as the nearby New Forest but many trees thrive within the woodland and there are clearings of arable land.

Stockbridge to Danebury Ring

Introduction: This walk combines the attractive countryside and spectacular downland of West Hampshire with a remarkable insight into the daily life of the Iron Age people who lived in this part of the Test Valley 2,000 years ago.

The route begins in Stockbridge, a famous fishing centre on the banks of the regal Test. With the handsome facade of the Grosvenor Hotel and its broad distinguished street of Tudor and Georgian houses, Stockbridge creates the impression of being a town of some size and importance although in reality it is a very small community. The walk then goes across country, with splendid views in all directions, to Danebury Ring, an Iron Age hill fort on the windswept downs above Stockbridge. Thousands of people come here every year to see this ancient and historic site and, if time permits, there is a mile-long trail which you can complete, illustrating the hill fort's fascinating background.

Distance: The route is just under 7 miles and should take about three hours to complete but allow a little longer to visit Danebury Ring and undertake the special trail there. Map: Ordnance Survey Landranger 185.

Refreshments: There are a number of public houses in and around Stockbridge. Bar food is available at The Grosvenor Hotel. The Old Three Cups Hotel offers morning coffee, bar snacks, lunch and dinner and a full English breakfast! The Peat Spade at Longstock serves bar meals.

How to get there: Stockbridge is about 8 miles south of Andover on the A30 Salisbury Road. Parking is easily available in the High Street.

The Walk: From the centre of Stockbridge head west following the main A30. Note the plaque by the bridge over the river. Cross the flowing waters of the Test and a few yards along the road to Houghton on the left is the Drovers' House. Apparently sheep drovers stayed the night here on their way to the Hampshire fairs from Wales. The inscription in Welsh on the front of the

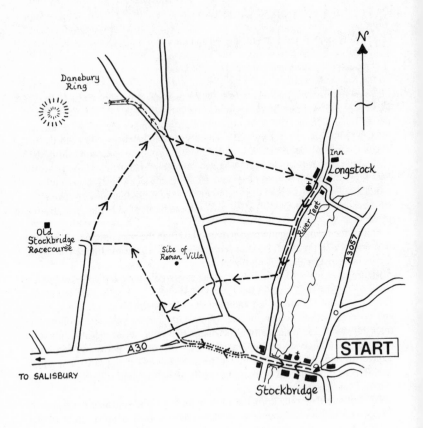

Danebury
Ring

N

Inn
Longstock

River Test

A3057

Old
Stockbridge
Racecourse

Site of
Roman Villa

A30

START

TO SALISBURY

Stockbridge

thatched house means seasoned hay, tasty pastures, good beer, comfortable beds!

Beyond the turning begin to climb the hill. When the A30 swings round to the right continue ahead along a quiet tarmac road signposted 'Roman Road'. After several yards it bears sharp left. Proceed ahead onto a narrow path running between thick banks of undergrowth. Continue for some minutes until you reach a stile in the right hand boundary. Take it and keep to the right hand edge of the field as far as the next stile and the main road. Cross the busy road with care to the stile in the opposite hedgerow.

Once over it walk ahead along the right hand edge of the field. Pass a stile on the right and continue ahead with open fields either side of you and fencing on your immediate right. Along this stretch there are fine views wherever you look. Keep to the field boundary and soon it dips into a fold. Proceed ahead up the other side and the fields on your right now mark the site of a Roman villa. You have a delightful uninterrupted view of Danebury Hill with its tuft of trees smudging the horizon. Continue ahead across the undulating farmland. In the field corner begin to head west and soon you reach the next field corner. Pass through the gap between the trees and hedgerows and turn sharp right onto a track. As you do so note the crumbling ivy-clad building almost enveloped by trees across the fields. This was the stadium of the old Stockbridge racecourse.

Follow the track, rough in places, until you reach the road after nearly a mile. In order to visit the hill fort, bear left and walk along the road until you reach the turning to Danebury Ring on the left.

Returning to the walk follow the road back to where the track you came down earlier joins the road. Avoid the track and continue along the road for a few yards past a turning on the left and then swing left onto a wide track with trees and undergrowth on your right and rolling farmland on your left. Follow the track for about 1½ miles noting the distinctive radio telescope at Chilbolton perched like a huge ice cream cornet on the far horizon. When you reach the village of Longstock continue down to the road and if you are in need of refreshment turn left and walk a few yards along the road to the delightfully named Peat Spade inn.

To continue the walk keep the church on the right and note a variety of houses, bungalows and colourwashed cottages along the main street of the village. Many of the gardens bordering the road are a delight to the eye during the spring and summer months − richly decorated with a profusion of different flowers and shrubs. Here also are some wonderful views of the river Test winding through the peaceful meadows away to your left. In places the famous fishermen's huts can be seen down by the water.

Continue along the road, clear of the houses of Longstock now, avoid a turning on the right and then after some minutes watch for a footpath sign on your right between a large field and a house called 'Butterflies'. Pass over the stile beside the sign and walk up the slope by keeping to the left hand boundary. When you reach the field corner pass through the sometimes-overgrown gap on your extreme left and then walk ahead to the next field boundary.

Again cross into the next field via the gap on your left. Continue ahead towards the farm buildings. Enter the concrete yard to the left of the buildings and then head towards the road. Pass through the gates and cross the road to a footpath sign where there are two gates. Go through the right hand gate into the field and then turn left and walk along its left hand boundary for some time until you reach the corner where there is a stile enabling you to cross into the field in front of you. All around you here are splendid views over windswept fields and downland. The scenery has a familiar look about it now and you will probably recall it from the initial stages of the walk.

Once over the stile turn left and proceed along the edge of the field to the main road. Cross over and go into the field opposite. Skirt it by the left hand edge until you reach the stile in the hedge. Pass over it and then turn left and walk along the leafy path back into Stockbridge where the walk began.

Historical Notes

Stockbridge: It is an important fishing centre with the impressive early 19th century Grosvenor Hotel in the High Street acting as the meeting place for those who hope that hours spent beside the tranquil waters of the Test prove to be fruitful. The hotel's ample and distinctive overhanging porch has become something of a local landmark in the town. It was built to prevent guests at the Grosvenor from getting wet as they arrived and departed in their carriages.

Near the town are over 200 acres of land which, with the lordship of the manor, are in the possession of the National Trust. Every March the manorial courts still meet and on these occasions a 17th century mace is exhibited. St Peter's church was built in 1865-66 after the old church fell into disrepair. It was rehallowed in 1963 and used as a mortuary chapel.

Stockbridge Racecourse: Until 1898 there was a racecourse here and for 150 years it was the venue for important meetings in the racing calendar. Then, at the end of the 19th century the racing switched to nearby Salisbury where there is still a racecourse today. The old building you can see across the fields was the stadium.

Danebury Ring: Now a public amenity area managed by Hampshire County Council recreation department, this was an important Iron Age hill fort covering an oval area of 13 acres. Cleverly constructed ditches and ramparts protected its inhabitants from invading forces. It is the largest and most intensively scrutinized prehistoric site in Britain. There are information panels at regular intervals illustrating the history of the hill fort. Danebury Ring is open every day. There is more information concerning the hill fort at the Museum of The Iron Age in Andover, open Tuesday to Saturday 10 am – 5 pm.

Longstock: The name of the public house here, The Peat Spade, comes from the tradition cultivated by local farmers of allowing their workers one day off a year to cut peat and then take it home in a cart loaned by their employer.

Near the village in the water meadows beside the Test there was once a 'Danish Dock'. The dock was created probably about 1,100 years ago for the Danes' flat-bottomed boats and was built in the form of a wide waterway or channel extending to about 300 ft.

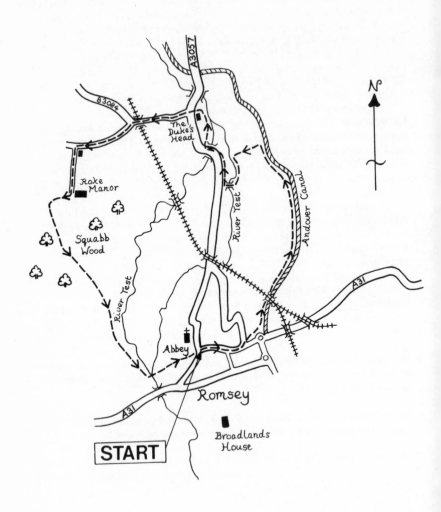

Romsey, the River Test and Squabb Wood

Introduction: The Test is known as the 'Queen of the Chalk Streams' and justly so for it is one of the most exclusive and expensive fishing rivers in the world as well as one of the most delightfully placid in Britain. Fed by clear springs under the chalk soil, the river is renowned for its trout fishing, though salmon is the fish of the lower Test. For some time the route of this walk runs alongside the river or near it.

The walk begins in Romsey, famous for its historic abbey ('the Lion of Hampshire') and its associations with two distinguished Englishmen, Admiral of the Fleet Earl Mountbatten of Burma and Lord Palmerston, Conservative Prime Minister during Queen Victoria's illustrious reign. Both men made their home here.

From Romsey the route follows the old Andover Canal before veering across country to the Duke's Head, a picturesque inn on the banks of the Test. The homeward stretch is along the Test Way through Squabb Wood, an extensive area of dense woodland carpeted with bracken. The last mile of the walk across open farmland offers splendid views of Romsey Abbey in the distance.

Distance: The walk is about 5¼ miles and should take about two and a half hours. Allow longer to visit Romsey Abbey and Broadlands. Map: Ordnance Survey Landranger 185.

Refreshments: Romsey has a number of town public houses offering bar meals. The Duke's Head, midway round the circuit, provides bar food.

How to get there: The walk begins in the market square in Romsey, which is located between Winchester and Southampton. There are several public car parks in the town.

The Walk: From the market square in Romsey make for Romsey Abbey, its imposing facade dominating the town centre.

Return to the market square and pass the statue of Lord Palmerston gazing out over the town that became his home. Go forward into The Hundred with the Corn Exchange on the right and follow it into Winchester Road. At the roundabout bear left, immediately before the Plaza Theatre, onto a footpath signposted Timsbury.

Follow the tarmac path beside the old Andover Canal which once ran from Andover to Redbridge near Southampton and was last in commercial use in 1874. This stretch is the longest water-filled section still in existence.

Pass under the railway bridge and continue beside the canal, heading in a general northerly direction through the outskirts of the town. Join a wider residential path and progress along the canal bank. Pass several footbridges and keep going, still with houses over on the left. Further on the path narrows. Proceed beyond another footbridge, go under a roadbridge and then you encounter a concrete bridge over the canal connecting a rough farm track. Soon there are views over pretty farmland and semi-wooded stretches of countryside. Pass under some pylons and continue ahead. There are several seats on this section of the walk for those wanting to pause and rest.

When you reach another bridge carrying a farm track over the canal, turn left onto a waymarked path and follow the left hand edge of the field with ditches either side of you and a line of trees on the left. In the corner veer right over a wooden footbridge into the trees. Follow the main path until you come to the banks of the Test and then bear left and walk alongside the river between lines of protective trees.

On reaching the grounds of a bungalow, proceed along the edge of the garden beside the river. Turn right at the bridge and follow the lane down to the road. Bear right and walk along the pavement beside the A3057. Follow the road as it curves left to a bridge over the Test. Cross the bridge and then veer right immediately onto a wooded path almost opposite the entrance to some pretty riverside cottages.

The water's edge is hard by you on the right now. (Take extra care along this stretch and if the river is high and the path waterlogged, keep to the main road as far as the Duke's Head.) Walk along the path through the trees. Soon, once clear of the trees, you come across a delightful view of the Test — the river flowing serenely through the gentle countryside. The waters of the Test are cool and crystal clear, its river plants swirling visibly beneath the surface. The setting is undeniably charming.

Pass a wooden footbridge with a sign 'Private — No Fishing' and continue along the riverbank. Go through a gate and walk along the edge of the garden of a private house until you reach a second gate. Turn left, pass through another gate and then join a drive leading to the house. Follow the drive away from the river until you reach the Duke's Head inn on the left.

From the inn cross over to the B3084 and follow it as it twists and turns through the countryside. Pass over the Salisbury-Southampton railway line and when the road swings right bear left into Old Salisbury Lane, signposted Roke Manor Research Centre and Stanbridge Earls School. The road climbs gradually between high hedges and banks. In a while it levels out before starting to rise gently again. On the flat once more continue until just beyond the entrance to Roke Manor and take the waymarked drive on the left.

Follow the drive past Roke Manor Farm and between hedgerows and when you reach the Research Centre's personnel department on the left and a car park on the right, proceed ahead for a few steps and then bear right onto a waymarked path which cuts across a rough field and can be quite overgrown in places. The vague outline of the route can be identified. Make your way to the far right hand corner of the field and cross the stile.

Once in the next field continue ahead towards the woodland and on reaching the trees pass through the obvious gap. Then swing left at once to follow the route of the Test Way through an area of sprawling unspoilt woodland known as Squabb Wood.

The path runs down to a stile and then continues through thick bracken. Keep to the main route, cross a footbridge and climb up between banks of trees, bracken and scrub. Soon you reach a major junction of clearly waymarked paths. Bear left here, still on the Test Way, following the signs for Romsey. Proceed through the heart of Squabb Wood watching for various symbols and arrows. The path undulates beneath the branches of delightful old beech trees and within sight of secret peaceful glades and bracken clearings.

When you reach an area of muddy, marshy ground swing left, cross a footbridge and continue on the main path. At length you pass over another footbridge followed by a stile. Keep to the path; there is a house on the left on this stretch. The direction of the Test Way is still clearly indicated by the various black arrows set against a white background on the tree trunks.

Cross over a stream by means of a footbridge with a stile at either end. Then pass over another stile and now you leave Squabb Wood and return to Romsey across a stretch of open farmland. Head diagonally right across the field towards the next stile. The squat tower of Romsey Abbey peeps into sight between the trees. Over to the right there are delightful views up to the wooded slopes of Burnt Grove beyond the A27.

Along the road about ½ mile to the west, though not visible from the walk, is Embley Park School, the family home of Florence Nightingale. Her grave is in the churchyard at nearby East Wellow and the obelisk there is inscribed with her initials 'FN'. She died in 1910 aged 90.

Cross a ditch and a stile followed by another stile and footbridge. Continue across the fields following the arrows and keeping the barbed wire fence beside you on the left. The bulk of Romsey Abbey remains in view over to the left. Aim for some buildings up ahead. On the left there is a particularly pretty view of the river Test meandering through the countryside — the delightful scene enhanced by the great edifice of the abbey over on the opposite bank.

On reaching the farm buildings negotiate a stile by a waymarker. After a few yards cross another stile and then continue with the river over to the left. When you reach the next stile by some houses proceed ahead passing a footpath on the right.

Swing left keeping to the track; this is still the Test Way. You will come to Saddlers Mill, where the salmon leap at the weir, an annual attraction among local people, when the fish return in the autumn to lay their eggs in the river. Bear left by the mill, leaving the route of the Test Way at last as it heads towards its most southerly point at Totton near Southampton.

Cross the river beside the mill following a tarmac path. Soon the route of the walk passes the War Memorial Park. Then it follows a residential road, passing a variety of property including elegant town houses, attractive villas and cottages before arriving at an arch and emerging into the market square where the walk began.

Historical Notes

Romsey: The market town became a borough in 1607 and since then it has boasted five town halls. At one time wool was the chief trade with several mills situated on the nearby streams of the Test. Later brewing became the key industry.

Apart from the abbey there are a number of interesting and historic buildings in the town, including the fine old Corn Exchange of 1864. King John's House in Church Street is mid 13th century and is apparently where his daughter resided before she married the King of Scotland. Subsequently, it became a guest house used by Romsey Abbey. It is open to the public.

Broadlands is famous for being the home of the late Earl Mountbatten of Burma until his death at the hands of IRA terrorists in 1979. Situated to the south of the town, overlooking the Test, it is an imposing porticoed house remodelled by 'Capability' Brown and John Holland in the mid 18th century.

Romsey Abbey: The great Norman church is one of the most impressive in Europe and certainly the finest in Hampshire. The abbey was founded in AD 907 by Edward the Elder, son of Alfred the Great, but the main part of the building, as it is today, was built in the 12th century by Henry de Blois,

Bishop of Winchester. Originally an Anglo-Saxon church stood on this site and the remains can be seen behind the choir screen.

Until the mid 16th century, Romsey Abbey was home to a Benedictine order of nuns; it is believed Edward's daughter may have been the first Abbess at Romsey for she is buried there. At the time of the Dissolution the abbey was saved from destruction by being sold to the people of Romsey for £100, whereupon it became the town's parish church.

The abbey is open daily between 9.30 am and 5.30 pm.

War Memorial Park: A haven of trees and flowers, the park was opened in 1920 as a memorial to the men who had died in battle. The 150 mm Japanese gun was captured by the 14th Army in Burma at the end of the Second World War and presented to the town by Earl Mountbatten when he became a Freeman of the Borough of Romsey.

TO SALISBURY

Hale

Hale
Park

Woodgreen

Densome
Corner

START

CP

Turf Hill
Inclosure

Godshill
Inclosure

Millersford
Bottom

Deadman Hill

B3078

B3080

New
Forest

A338

N

TO BOURNEMOUTH

Woodgreen in the New Forest

Introduction: The New Forest is the jewel in Hampshire's crown. The largest remaining unspoilt medieval forest in western Europe, it has a unique atmosphere and a distinctive character. Once a royal preserve, it is a romantic place of ancient dark legends and historic literary associations.

Though this great legacy, like all our national beauty spots, is under threat from the pressure of modern day tourists and holidaymakers, many people who visit the forest never venture more than a few yards from the many car parks. They remain unaware that beyond lies a vast wooded landscape; a haven for plants and wildlife including deer, badgers and foxes. A peaceful place in a crowded hectic world. This walk has been chosen to take advantage of one of the lesser-known corners of this delightful region, exploring the forest's hidden depths as it journeys along quiet woodland paths interspersed with tracts of open heathland and plain. The walk heads for Godshill Inclosure and its lovely mixed woods of oaks, beeches, pines and sweet chestnuts before making for the village of Woodgreen. The village green is a notable feature and ideal for rest and refreshment. The community hall at Woodgreen displays murals representing village life down the years.

Distance: This is a circuit of 7 miles and should take about three hours to complete. Map: Ordnance Survey Landranger 184.

Refreshments: The Horse and Groom at Woodgreen offers bar snacks at lunchtime and in the evening. Summer puddings are a noted speciality!

How to get there: From the M27 at Junction 1 join the B3078 Fordingbridge road. After about 4 miles, at the fork, turn right onto the B3080 and the turning to Turf Hill Inclosure, where the walk begins, is on the left. The car park can be busy.

The Walk: From the car park at Turf Hill Inclosure proceed to the far end of the parking area and join a path between wooden posts. Follow the path through the bracken and pass a small pond on the left. Continue ahead with excellent views to the south west over an unspoilt landscape comprising beautiful woodland and open heath.

Carry on along the main path as it curves to the left and down the slope. At the bottom, beside the fence post, turn sharp right and keep the trees on your right. Further on there is a gentle upward slope. Continue in a westerly direction up to the top of the incline and then down the other side as the path heads out across one of the many delightful heathland expanses to be found within the boundaries of the New Forest. Avoid turnings on the left and right and proceed ahead. At this early stage of the walk look out for a small clump of pine trees on the slopes of the hillside over on the near horizon. The path climbs again and when it levels out join a broad grassy ride with trees on the right.

Soon the ride drops down to provide glorious vistas ahead. As you descend the slope the path forks. Take the left turning with the pines clearly visible a little to the left across the Millersford valley. When you reach a junction of paths level with the pine trees on the left hand hillside, turn left and pass over the little stream running along Millersford Bottom. Follow the path up the hill keeping to the right of the pines. From the edge of this delightful little spinney, handy for a brief bit of cooling shade on a hot summer's day, there are glorious views back across the Millersford valley towards Turf Hill Inclosure and the start of this lovely walk.

Beyond the trees the path climbs steeply up the bank to reach the car park at Deadman Hill, a local beauty spot with fine views in all directions. As you approach the road swing right onto a path and note Hampton Ridge ahead of you standing out clearly on the horizon. At the road turn right and follow the springy grassy path beside the B3078. Pass over several cattle grids and look out for a solitary tree on the right of the road. Continue beyond the tree and very soon you reach a wire fence on the right opposite a car park. Veer right, leave the road and follow the path running along the right hand edge of the fence between banks of gorse and bracken.

A little further along the path there are glorious glimpses of woodland over to the west beyond the fence. Ahead of you on the near horizon as you descend the steep slope are the trees of Godshill Inclosure. Further down the path runs alongside a ragged line of trees on the left. In a minute or two the walk drops down to a stream which unfortunately lacks a footbridge. As the stream is quite wide here it is advisable to turn right and walk briefly amidst the trees and undergrowth until you reach a point where it is easier to cross. On the opposite bank rejoin the main path. Further up, it veers left towards a pine tree. Follow the path as it climbs up between banks of bracken. From the higher ground looking back you can see the clump of pine trees of earlier as well as the general route of the path so far, including Turf Hill Inclosure and the surrounding area.

Follow the path across to the car park at Godshill Inclosure and make for the gate amid the trees on the right. This is Gate Number 4; the accompanying notice advises us that walkers 'may use this access for the purpose of peaceful enjoyment of air and exercise but are reminded that it is not a public right of way'. The route here is along a permitted path by kind permission of the Forestry Commission.

Follow the wide path through the bracken and trees. Cross a gravelled track and immediately the path forks. Take the right fork and progress through dense dark woodland carpeted with undergrowth and bracken. This is the heart of Godshill Inclosure. Keep on the path. Pass over a cross track and progress between the trees. Further down the slope the route joins another path and continues in the same direction through the trees. Now the walk descends into a truly unspoilt part of the forest, a secret place of lovely overhanging beech trees and cooling breezes.

On reaching another path on a U shaped bend proceed ahead, avoiding the turning on the extreme right. Follow the main path between trees and bracken. When you reach a gate emerge from the trees onto the delightful village green at Woodgreen. The green is lined with houses and picturesque thatched cottages creating a charming picture and on the far horizon beyond the dwellings the downs of South Wiltshire are clearly visible. The green is ideal for a break as there are several seats to be found hereabouts. Note, too, the pretty thatched pavilion located alongside the boundary. Within the green is the village cricket pitch enclosed by fencing. Pass to the side of the pitch and on reaching the road bear left.

Walk down the lane keeping houses on the right and the village green on the left. Follow the road as far as the junction and here on the left is the Horse and Groom. On the right is Woodgreen church room built in 1914; the church of St Boniface. Next to it is Woodgreen village hall.

Retrace your steps back up the road and across the green into Godshill Inclosure once more. Follow the path down the slope through the trees and at the U shaped bend continue ahead between the cooling beeches. Avoid the turning on the right from earlier and now you are once again covering new ground. Pass a cross track and continue ahead. Along this stretch in the verges grows the distinctive yellowish mushroom, chanterelle.

After several minutes or so, when you reach another track, turn left for a few yards and then bear right at a junction of tracks and join a path running through thick woodland. Follow the path until you reach Gate 2. Emerge from the trees at the roadside by a house on the right. This is Densome Corner forming part of the New Forest boundary. If time permits you can follow the road to Hale and glimpse the imposing facade of Hale Park; alternatively you may wish to use the OS map to reach the village across the fields. There are several footpaths.

Returning to Densome Corner take the track beside the house noting the sign 'Access to Wild Close only'. Follow the track down into the trees. As you do so look out once more for the familiar pine spinney rapidly becoming one of the key features of this walk and serving as a very useful directional landmark. Keep on the track through the trees and between banks of scrub. At length it veers a little to the right by a field gate and a ditch on the left. Follow it, passing between clumps of bushes and gorse and after a few steps the pine trees come into view again on the right. Follow the path and you will see that the route is once again through the Millersford Valley.

Begin the final leg of the walk by crossing the stream, but now instead of retracing your steps back to the car park at Turf Hill Inclosure swing left away from the pines following a clear path close to the trees on the left. Aim for some gate posts up ahead in the line of trees. Here the wide path cuts between regimented rows of pine trees. Follow the path as it curves left and take the second right hand turning opposite another path running into the trees.

Stay on the path and head up the side of the hill. When the path levels out continue between rows of pine trees for a while. In due course merge with another path and continue ahead. At the end of the plantations with a line of pylons visible up ahead, swing right onto a broad grassy ride running along the edge of the trees. In a few moments when the trees end veer a little to the left along a path running parallel with the pylons and heading towards a clump of pine trees at Turf Hill Inclosure where the walk started. Very soon the car park is reached.

Historical Notes

New Forest: The word 'forest' conjures up images of wild, uncultivated tracts of land and extensive dense woodland. In medieval times that is precisely how the New Forest was made up. Today, apart from the obvious intrusion of 20th century commercialism, the forest has changed little since William the Conqueror established it as his deer park.

The 20-mile stretch of the forest comprises more than 90,000 acres extending roughly from the south coast to the Wiltshire border. The variety of landscape is immense and among the many species of trees are beech, oak and chestnut.

Woodgreen is close to the river Avon and lies along the western boundary of the New Forest. The community hall, unusually, has walls covered with fascinating murals depicting life in the village. The hall was built in the early

1930s and it was then that two young artists, Ted Payne and Robert Baker, hit upon the idea of creating a unique sociological record of the time. It is all wonderfully evocative, recalling a way of life that, sadly, has all but disappeared in the so-called march of progress.

Hale Park is a splendid Georgian porticoed mansion designed by the architect Thomas Archer when he bought the estate in 1715, though some alterations were made towards the end of the 18th century. Beyond the house lies Archer's 18th century church. He is buried in the family vault. The approach to Hale Park is impressive; a long elegant avenue of trees leads to the house from the lodge. Hale Park is not open to the public.

Keyhaven and Pennington Marshes

Introduction: The coastal village of Keyhaven, where this interesting walk begins, is a quiet outpost looking across the Solent to the Isle of Wight and situated on the edge of a marsh landscape more reminiscent perhaps of East Anglia than Hampshire.

These salt marshes and the flocks of geese and migratory birds that inhabit them provide the backdrop for much of this walk. For a while the route follows the Solent Way, near where this long distance footpath starts at Milford-on-Sea, with spectacular views across to the Isle of Wight. Passing shipping and colourful sails can easily be spotted from here. At length it heads away from the coast to reach a charming old inn, The Chequers, at the halfway point. The return leg offers constant glimpses of the Solent and the Needles on the horizon.

If time permits there is the option of extending the walk at Keyhaven as far as Hurst Castle, a historic fort open to the public and occupying a superb coastal position at the end of a long pebble spit. You can then return to Keyhaven by ferry, depending on sailing times.

Distance: About two hours should be allowed for this walk of 5¼ miles. This does not include the spur to Hurst Castle. Map: Ordnance Survey Landranger 196.

Refreshments: The Gun at Keyhaven provides bar food. The Chequers at Pennington has real ale and bar meals; seafood is among a number of different dishes available.

How to get there: From Lymington or Christchurch take the A337 and then turn onto the B3058 Milford-on-Sea road. Keyhaven is signposted and on reaching the village, park opposite The Gun. This car park is the starting point for the circuit.

The Walk: From the car park in the centre of Keyhaven take the adjacent road immediately opposite Hawker's Cottage. Go over the bridge and then when you reach a sign 'No vehicles beyond 200 yards ahead', turn right onto a waymarked footpath and follow the sea wall around the perimeter of Keyhaven harbour with its colourful boats and bustling air. From here there are magnificent views across to the slender white column of Hurst Castle lighthouse and in the distance, off the south west corner of the Isle of Wight, the serrated, white-tipped rocks of the Needles which, together with the lighthouse, have long been one of the island's chief attractions.

Keep on the path following the route of the Solent Way for a while. The long distance path of 60 miles begins in nearby Milford-on-Sea and concludes at Emsworth just to the east of Portsmouth. The route was devised by Hampshire County Council and opened in 1982.

Head out across Keyhaven Marshes with its lagoons and mudflats and here again there are superb views of the Isle of Wight seemingly only a stone's throw across the Solent. From the path virtually the entire western coast of the island is clearly visible, particularly on a good sunny day. Without doubt it is an impressive sight.

Follow the path along the sea wall and eventually it curves towards a promontory. On reaching the sharp point follow it round to the left and then continue across this lonely landscape. Flooding has long been a problem on this stretch of the Hampshire coast though the sea wall came too late to stop the salterns (shallow ponds of salt water) from being destroyed in some places, demonstrating the vital need for protection.

When you reach a sign warning of quicksand out among the mudflats, start to swing left away from the foreshore and join a path immediately opposite the jetty. Pass through the opening and continue on the straight track over Pennington Marshes, still with distant views of the Needles over to the left. On reaching the information panels at the next gate go through the gap at the side and turn right following the narrow lane. When the road bends sharp left look out for a waymarked footpath about 50 yards beyond the bend.

Take the path running between wire fences and after a few yards it becomes enclosed by trees and hedgerows. Keep on the main path and pass Oxey Farm house after a few minutes. Join the road and follow it round to the right passing various houses and cottages. Soon the road bears left. Continue along it noting Creek Cottage on the right. When you reach Chequers Green on the left proceed ahead to the Chequers inn, also on the left. The building dates back to the 16th century and was the local salt exchange. Soon after the pub there is Poles Lane on the right and just beyond it a waymarked footpath on the left. Cross the stile and follow the somewhat overgrown path to another stile. Once over it, continue ahead across the field and then at the next stile cross over and turn left through the gap in the hedgerow. Swing right, through the grass and scrub. On reaching another stile go forward to join a wide gravelled driveway leading to Oakhaven Hospice. Follow the drive to the road.

Cross over and take the drive in front of you, passing to the right of a house and its outbuildings. Proceed to the end of the drive and then continue across the lawn as far as the stile. Go over it and turn right following a track. After about 50 yards bear left when the track swings right. On reaching a gate go round the side of it and continue along the grassy track. Avoid turnings left and right and keep following the main track.

Along this stretch there are teasing glimpses of the Isle of Wight and the Solent across to the Needles. At the road turn left and walk along its metalled surface looking for the slim outline of Hurst Castle lighthouse just below the spectacular island horizon.

On reaching the buildings of the waste tip veer right onto a public footpath heading back towards Keyhaven. Follow the track between the fields keeping the lighthouse, a very useful landmark, within your sights. At length the path arrives at a junction with a stile and footpath. Continue ahead and on reaching a gate edge round the side of it and follow the road. Soon the buildings of Keyhaven come into view. Pass the route of the Solent Way on your left at the point where it begins to follow the sea wall around the edge of Keyhaven harbour and return to the car park where the walk began.

The spur to Hurst Castle: Having admired the scene from afar, an optional extra 1½ mile walk along Hurst Spit to Hurst Castle and its neighbouring lighthouses, one tall and white and recognisable for miles around, the other a low and less conspicuous structure, is well worthwhile if time permits.

Walking along the pebble beach is wearisome at times, particularly in rough weather when the sea is like a boiling cauldron though the waves breaking a few feet from you can be a spectacular sight. The effort is worth it, however, for Hurst Castle is a fascinating building and from it the views of the Isle of Wight are outstanding. The island is so close that it has the appearance of being just across a wide river or an estuary at this point.

You can return to Keyhaven by ferry (summer only) which after the arduous trek along the spit provides the opportunity to travel back to the mainland at a comfortable leisurely pace.

Historical Notes

Keyhaven: The village witnessed scenes of controversy before the First World War when plans were drawn up to create a tunnel from here to the Isle of Wight. There was also a proposal to build a docks development on the marshes to the east of Keyhaven. Thankfully for the local residents, neither plan came to fruition.

Pennington Marshes: Together with Lymington and Keyhaven this coastal expanse includes salt and freshwater marshes and mudflats stretching from the Lymington river in the east as far as Hurst Spit to the west.

Once, this area played a key role in the salt industry and, despite its decline in the mid 19th century there is still evidence, here and there, of such activity.

Above all, these marshes represent a haven for wildlife including various species of nesting bird and in the summer months terns are drawn here from as far afield as Southern Africa and the Antarctic. Other species come here from northern Scandinavia, northern Russia and Iceland.

Hurst Castle: One of Henry VIII's forts, it was built in the 1540s to defend the western entrance to the Solent when the threat of coastal invasion was at its peak. It was here that Charles I was held prisoner for two weeks in 1648 having been captured at Carisbrooke Castle on the Isle of Wight.

It is now in the care of English Heritage and is open to the public from Easter until the end of September, daily between 10 am and 6 pm, and from the beginning of October until Easter, weekends only 10 am to 4 pm. The ferry service operates between mid May and October.

Bursledon and the Royal Victoria Country Park

Introduction: The shores of Southampton Water conceal hidden pockets of unspoilt countryside and commonland. Here and there one can still stumble on picturesque creeks and attractive woodland and this route explores these hidden depths, offering the walker a great deal of variety along the way. Beginning in the yachting village of Bursledon the walk heads for the river, passing close to the well known Jolly Sailor inn. From here the walk goes across country to the historic village of Hamble. Beyond it is a spectacular stretch following the Solent Way beside the busy shipping lanes of Southampton Water.

At last we reach the Royal Victoria Country Park, one of the major highlights of this walk. Overlooking the wide waterway, this peaceful park was once the site of a huge military hospital. Only the chapel remains, with its splendid dome visible during much of the walk.

Distance: This is a walk of about 8 miles. It should take four hours but allow longer to look around Hamble and visit the Royal Victoria Country Park including the exhibition and the war graves cemetery. Map: Ordnance Survey Landranger 196.

Refreshments: The Jolly Sailor and The Vine at Bursledon serve a good range of bar food and the former also has an a la carte restaurant. In Hamble there are several inns. The Victory serves bar meals and morning coffee, and The King and Queen also does food. The Bugle is Hamble's famous waterfront restaurant and public house; seafood is a speciality here. The Old Whyte Hart Inn provides country fare. The Village Tearooms offer morning coffee, light lunches and afternoon teas.

How to get there: Bursledon is just off the M27 (Junction 8) to the west of Southampton and a little to the south of the A27 and the A3024. The walk starts at the free car park by the railway station.

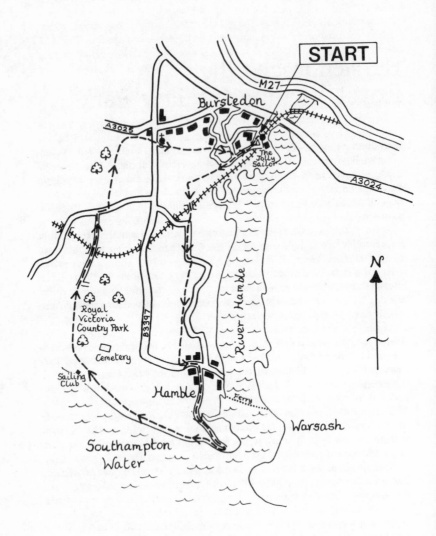

The Walk: From the car park at Bursledon follow the sign for the Jolly Sailor and climb up the steep path. At the top join the road. To reach the inn veer left at the fork and then left at the junction. The entrance is a short distance along the road and access is via some steps leading down to the water. The Jolly Sailor is more than just a pub. Its setting below road level, sheltered by trees behind, and directly overlooking the Hamble is surely one of the most unusual and fascinating to be found anywhere in this part of the country.

From the inn retrace your steps along the road but instead of turning off at the junction proceed ahead with Dale Cottage on the left and Yew Tree Cottage on the right. Further along the road there is a narrow gateway on the left through which is a delightful viewpoint erected by kind permission of the landowner. Using the information panel you can learn about the history and background of the Lower Hamble valley where the Hamble winds between thickly wooded banks towards its estuary overlooking Southampton Water. From here on a good day you can look across to St Catherine's Hill 20 miles away on the far side of the Isle of Wight. Over to the right is the tall slender chimney of Fawley power station.

Returning to the road, continue ahead and on reaching a telephone box turn left and follow the High Street, noting The Vine inn on the left. Pass Salterns Lane and proceed ahead. As the road veers right go forward onto a waymarked path to the right of a property called Arne. Pass a footpath on the right to Hamble and continue ahead onto a tarmac drive. After about 75 yards the drive veers right by Hungerford End. Proceed ahead onto a wooded path between this property and Woodlands, a bungalow on the left.

Descend a steep slope between the trees and beyond a drive leading to a white cottage follow the clear path through the woodland. The path climbs between trees and banks of bracken. Avoid a right turning and when the path levels out continue to a drive. Bear right for several yards before swinging half left between some oak trees. A path is visible over by a high wire fence. Join the path and follow it with the fence hard on your left. On the distant horizon is the distinctive dome of the chapel in the Royal Victoria Country Park which from time to time acts as a very useful landmark on this walk. Follow the path to the left. Pass over the railway line via the bridge and then reach the road by the entrance to Wessex House and Manor.

Continue ahead along the road and soon it swings left. After several minutes look for a footpath on the right just beyond a 'private — no footpath' sign. Take the path and follow it between wire fences with good views over towards the yachts of Hamble and the wooded slopes beyond. Further on there are suburban houses and gardens on the left. At the top of a slope the path broadens out to a wide band of grass. Proceed beyond some garages and then join a residential road. Pass Meadow Lane on the left and go on to the road junction. Turn left and walk down the lane into the village of Hamble, passing School Lane on the right.

After a brief stroll along the pretty Hamble riverbank and perhaps a little refreshment in one of the many inns here, retrace your steps to School Lane. Follow the lane and when you reach its junction with Copse Lane swing left, still in School Lane. Pass a sign 'Welcome to Hamble Common'. As the information panel tells you, Henry VIII's famous flagship 'Mary Rose' was lost in a furious battle near here with the loss of 700 men.

Just beyond the sign join a footpath on the left running parallel with the road, though in places screened from it by a thick curtain of trees and vegetation. At length you reach the road at the entrance to Hamble Point Marina emerging from the enclosed path on the edge of breezy Southampton Water. The change in scenery is abrupt to say the least with spectacular views across this majestic waterway. On the opposite bank is Fawley oil refinery and a little to the left beyond Calshot spit the low sprawling outline of the Isle of Wight looking like some huge basking sea monster on the horizon. The great warships of old no longer ply these waters but today the scene is still colourful and hectic. You don't have to wait long to spot an oil tanker, a tug or a Red Funnel ferry. The low roar of the sleek hydrofoil may arouse your interest too as it zips in and out of Southampton docks. There is always something worth seeing on Southampton Water.

From the marina entrance walk away along the shoreline towards Netley and Southampton keeping the waterway on your left. Almost at once you come upon the Second World War gun emplacement. Follow the path through the gorse and when you reach the boundary fence of BP Oil's Hamble terminal continue ahead along the sea wall. You are now following part of the Solent Way. Beyond the depot join the beach briefly and glancing to your right note the line of houses on the outskirts of Hamble. When you reach a concrete fortification turn right onto a path leading through the gorse into the trees. On reaching the road bear left passing the 'Westfield Common' sign. Keep to the road with glimpses of Southampton Water on the left and on the right, beyond the fence, the grounds of British Aerospace.

When you reach a junction of ways proceed ahead to the right of Hamblecliff House. Follow the drive between wire fences towards the entrance to Hamblecliff Stables. Take the narrow path to the left of the gate. This is still the Solent Way and a sign on this stretch advises you that this is a permitted path.

The path cuts through an area of trees and scrub with the boats of Netley Sailing Club visible on the left. Soon the path swings right and runs up a slope into some woods. Emerging from the trees onto a wide grassy expanse you are now on the edge of the Royal Victoria Country Park.

Aim for the front of the chapel with its famous green dome and note the plaque on an adjacent wall to the right of the entrance. If time allows you may like to relax in the park; its trees and delightful green spaces provide the perfect opportunity to do so. You might also want to spend a little time in the war graves cemetery located in a peaceful glade in the north east corner of the old hospital grounds. There is also the Empire tearoom if refreshment is desired.

To resume the main walk go past the public convenience beside the tearoom and continue almost as far as the car park. Just before it veer right onto a stony path. Follow the path with the car park now on your left and when you reach a junction of ways continue ahead following the sign 'no vehicular access'. Proceed along the metalled drive as it curves right and on reaching the barrier go forward past Hound Lodge onto Hound Road. Continue over the railway line past some houses and bungalows and when you reach the road junction turn right. Walk along the road for about 50 yards and then cross over by a bus stop and take the waymarked footpath opposite.

Descend the slope onto the route of the old road and continue ahead keeping the newer road parallel on the right. Pass the entrance to a house on the left; the path becomes a narrow strip at this point as it cuts through banks of thick scrub. The route here tends to be somewhat overgrown in high summer. After a few yards bear left to a stile in the boundary. Cross over into the field and then swing left following the field edge. On reaching the stile in the next field boundary go over it and continue with woodland on the left. Cross another stile and glancing back at this stage reveals one final glimpse of the chapel dome at Netley, a pleasant lasting reminder of the historic site and its quiet unspoilt surroundings. On the left at this point is a path running down to a lake in a secluded setting amid overhanging trees. It is peaceful and undiscovered here − hard to believe that the sprawling urban environs of Southampton and the south coast towns are so close.

Return to the path and continue along the field edge. In the corner go forward where the path cuts between scrub and root crops. Follow the path round to the right and cross a field of rough pasture, ignoring a turning on the left. Head towards a line of houses and on reaching the main road cross over into Chamberlayne Road opposite; this is the outskirts of Bursledon. Keep to the road as it swings right, past St Paul's church on the left. Pass Nightingale Road and Foundry Crescent on the left and follow the road round to the right. When you reach the junction bear left. At the end of the road beneath a smattering of trees go forward to join a waymarked path. Cross a footbridge over a stream, then go over a quiet residential road and continue on the next section of path between hedgerows. Now it begins a gradual pull before rapidly becoming much steeper. At the top join a road and proceed ahead for about 75 yards. Then bear left onto a waymarked path passing through a gate. Follow the path between fields and fences. On reaching the road turn right passing a property called Ladymead on the right. On the left now is Greyladyes with the little Roman Catholic chapel of Our Lady of the Rosary and its Gothic belfry.

At the next junction veer left and follow the road back into Bursledon. Turn left opposite Dale Cottage and either the steep path or the road will bring you back to the car park beside the station.

Historical Notes

Bursledon is divided into two distinct parts — new and old. The latter is the more interesting, its period buildings clinging to the banks of the river Hamble. Here, the village still retains the air of an unspoilt romantic river community despite the tourists and the forest of masts.

Between the 14th and early 19th centuries, Bursledon was an important centre for naval shipbuilding. The wooded slopes fringing the river provided much of the timber. HMS Elephant, Nelson's 74 gun flagship at the battle of Copenhagen, was built here by George Parsons and launched at his yard in August 1786. The Elephant boatyard is named after the ship.

Hamble: Situated at the broad mouth of the river, it is a quaint place of steep winding streets and pretty cottages, likened by Pevsner to a West Country fishing village. Famous as a yachting centre, Hamble has long thrived on its close proximity to the river with its shipbuilding, yacht clubs and marinas. Originally just a small fishing village renowned for oysters, crabs and lobsters, Hamble was later to become a sprawling community with the accent on leisure and aircraft industry. The college of Air Training is nearby as is the British Aerospace factory. One of Britain's first aviators, Sir Alliott Verdon-Roe is buried in the partly Norman church. St Andrew's was the church of the Benedictine priory of Hamble-le-Rice founded in 1109. There are quite a few pubs in Hamble including The Bugle. The riverside inn probably dates from the 12th century. A sign on the wall facing the river explains the history in a little more detail. There is a daily ferry service from here across the Hamble to Warsash on the opposite bank.

Royal Victoria Country Park: The surviving chapel is indeed a worthy memorial to the home of Army nursing, once the country's greatest military hospital.

It was Queen Victoria who argued the need for such a hospital to minister to the sick and injured casualties of war following reports of the dreadful conditions in the Crimea. The 220 acre site at Netley overlooking Southampton Water was purchased in January 1856 and in May that year Queen Victoria laid the foundation stone, beneath which lay a prototype of the newly instituted VC decoration, 'for valour', and a Crimean medal. When completed, the hospital was ¼ mile long, so large that it would be hard to imagine such a place being built today. Netley included a thousand beds and cost more than £300,000 to construct. The hospital was completed too late to play a role in the Crimean war though for the next 100 years it contributed to the medical welfare of thousands of fighting men. The sick, dying and injured were brought here from the far-flung, war-torn corners of the British Empire.

The hospital included a 570 ft long pier, opened in 1868 and intended to speed up the process of carrying casualties ashore from the troop ships instead of bringing them to Netley by road from Southampton. Horse-drawn ambulances ferried the stretcher cases from the pier head straight into the hospital. Later, hospital ships took over and the victims of war were brought to Netley by train − arriving at the hospital's very own station.

In 1966, despite resistance, the hospital was demolished with only the chapel remaining intact. During the demolition the VC was discovered under the foundation stone. The chapel at the centre of the hospital was where wounded soldiers dressed in uniform united with medical staff to pray and worship together. It was capable of accommodating 900 people.

In 1980 the site of the hospital was bought by Hampshire County Council who subsequently transformed it into a most attractive country park. Here amid the grassy expanses it is possible to identify the boundaries of the old building. Inside the chapel is an exhibition dedicated to the history of Netley and which conveys quite eerily a little of the atmosphere of those tragic days.

The park is open throughout the year. The Royal Victoria Centre in the chapel is open between 12 midday−5 pm on weekdays and 10 am−5 pm on Sundays. Last entry 4.30 pm.

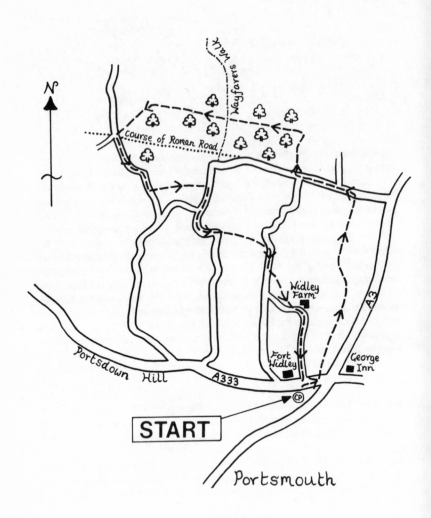

N

Wayfarers Walk

Course of Roman Road

Widley Farm

Fort Widley

George Inn

Portsdown Hill   A333

CP

START

Portsmouth

A3

Portsdown Hill
and the Wayfarer's Walk

Introduction: Portsdown Hill, a famous chalk ridge and one of the most fascinating geological features on the south coast, marks the start of this walk. From the top the views of Portsmouth are breathtaking with the whole of this world-famous naval city, known affectionately as 'Pompey' to seamen and football supporters alike, spread out beneath you on Portsea Island.

On top of the hill where wild, chalk-loving flowers and plants grow in profusion the walk turns its back on Portsmouth to head north along the Wayfarer's Walk, a long distance footpath, and here the contrast between the spectacular views at the start and the subsequent wooded stretches is truly memorable. The route passes close to Southwick House which played a key role in the final outcome of the Second World War. The house was the Supreme Allied Headquarters and here General Eisenhower and the Allied chiefs launched their invasion of Europe on 6th June, 1944 – D-Day.

The walk returns to Portsdown Hill where there is the chance to extend the route by taking the Fort Widley trail which runs alongside this landmark. The various information panels give an interesting insight into its history and its role in the defence of the Hampshire coast.

Distance: The circuit is about 5 miles. Allow two to two and a half hours though an additional 30 minutes or thereabouts should be set aside for the Fort Widley trail. Map: Ordnance Survey Landranger 196.

Refreshments: The George Inn is only a couple of minutes on foot from the main route of the walk and offers a lunchtime menu. To reach it head east from the viewpoint car park along the main road and the pub is on the left.

How to get there: The viewpoint car park where the walk begins is at the top of Portsdown Hill. Take the A3 London-Portsmouth road and follow the signs.

The Walk: From the viewpoint car park high above Portsmouth, head in an easterly direction along the A333 keeping the extensive views of the city and its sprawling suburbs on your right. From here you can spot Gosport, the dockyard, the continental ferry terminal and the old city lying at the entrance to Portsmouth Harbour.

Begin to descend the slope towards the George Inn and then cross over to the opposite footpath signposted Dellcrest Path. Join the path, part of the Wayfarer's Walk, a 70 mile route running the length of Hampshire from Emsworth to the Berkshire border near Newbury, and after a few yards when it veers right towards an assortment of houses and bungalows continue down between banks of scrub with a wire fence on the left. There are good views ahead of you over towards the southern fringes of the Forest of Bere.

Further down the slope, the path runs directly alongside a row of suburban gardens on the right while the scene on the left is made up of fields and hedgerows. At the end of the line of houses the path swings left. Keep on it with a hedgerow on the right and fields on the left. There are good views, too, to the south stretching to the ridge of Portsdown Hill and the outline of the polygonal forts situated along the spine of the hill.

Shortly the path veers right into a thin belt of trees and bushes. Further on the woodland becomes a little broader. Continue ahead in a northerly direction. Cross over a stream via a wooden footbridge. A little beyond it you reach a white gate and a stile. Cross over and proceed up the drive between several houses on the left and a cricket ground and tennis court on the right. On reaching the road pause for a few moments to glance back to the ridge of Portsdown Hill still standing out clearly on the southerly horizon. Turn left and walk down the road. When it turns right continue ahead along a quiet country lane between trees and hedgerows. Pass the gate lodge at the entrance to Purbrook Heath House on the right, then a turning on the left and just beyond it turn right onto a path running along the edge of a patch of woodland with a field on the left. Within a couple of minutes or so the path enters a dense wood. Proceed through the trees and when you reach the far side cross a stile and then turn right and follow the edge of a large corn field. In the field corner go over a second stile and then follow the path through a smattering of trees into the next field. Farm buildings are visible up ahead.

Bear left and walk along the field edge until you reach the corner and then join a path and turn left heading back towards the field you were in a few moments earlier! The route of the path tends to meander during this stage of the walk.

A row of pylons can be seen just ahead of you now. Cross the field beneath the pylons and when you pass into the next field bear right towards an area of woodland. Follow the perimeter of the field along a clear path with the trees on the right and crops on the left. After about 200 yards or so you will see a stile in the right hand boundary. Cross the stile and follow the path into the trees, cutting deep into the heart of this thick deciduous woodland. The path, lined with clusters of bracken, is boggy in places.

After several minutes you reach a major junction of paths with the Wayfarer's Walk crossing our route as indicated by the wooden post. Note the small plaque which reads: 'Presented by Dr and Mrs M.A. Bridgewood of Clemson USA and erected by Ramblers' Association Meon Group, 17th July 1982'. On the left here is a delightful avenue of tall fir trees.

Continue ahead across the route of the Wayfarer's Walk going deeper into the wood. Keep on the main path through the trees and the various clearings. The ground is a carpet of undergrowth and bracken and here and there fallen trees are clearly visible. When the path forks, veer right and then after a few yards go right again in a clearing heading towards the edge of the wood. The path twists and turns and at length reaches the woodland boundary. Cross a ditch and then bear immediately left along a narrow path between the trees with glorious views on the right over open countryside.

Negotiate a stile and then walk down to the field corner where there is a ford or cattle crossing. In order to cross it look for a gap in the trees on the left of it and then pass over the footbridge. On the other side of the bridge is a stile which you should take. Head across the field to the next stile and then continue ahead to the stile in the hedge beside the road. Looking back half right at this point you may care to imagine the route of a Roman road which once ran across this landscape from Chichester to Winchester. Though there are no visible signs of it today the Ordnance Survey map identifies its course. Nearby to the west lies the historic village of Southwick.

Once over the stile bear left and follow the road. Soon it curves left and there is a gentle slope on this stretch. The road is lined with bracken margins and on the right of you is a burst of woodland. Keep on the road as it veers right; pass a footpath on the right. When you reach a farm on the right turn left over a stile onto a waymarked path and head up the field paddock to the top apex. Cross the stile into the next field and proceed ahead over this high breezy ground with very good views of the ridge of Portsdown Hill over to the right. All around you at this stage of the walk is a rolling carpet of fields, hedgerows and trees as far as the eye can see.

Aim for the gap on the far side of the field. Pass through it, go over a stile and then, on reaching the edge of the next field after several yards, walk along the left hand boundary keeping the woodland on the left. Follow the field edge and when you reach the corner cross the stile out into the road. Turn right and walk down the lane between trees and banks of bracken. Soon the road swings right. Continue downhill and when it bears sharp right go straight on following the left hand curve. Then, as it begins gradually to veer right, look out for a footpath sign on the left situated a few yards from the road on the other side of the ditch. The sign is not apparent from the road as it is hidden behind a curtain of bushes and scrub. Cross the little ditch and join the path leading to the sign and the accompanying stile. Go over the stile and proceed ahead along the left edge of the field. On reaching the field corner continue forward into the undergrowth and then cross into the next field via a stile. Head straight across the field, passing beneath the power lines and aim for a gate and stile up ahead located to the left of a farm.

Cross the stile, go forward a few yards to the next stile and the waymarker and cross out to the road. Turn right and follow the road as it swings right after a few yards. Pass a footpath sign on the left and continue along the road. After several minutes bear left over a stile onto a waymarked path with a line of telegraph poles marching briskly up to the ridge. Veer diagonally right across this field to the far corner. Pass through the opening into the next field and after several yards bear right onto a track. Turn left following the track towards the buildings of Widley Farm.

Swing to the right of the buildings, still on the track, and when you reach the junction opposite a bungalow bear right. Proceed up the hill on a clear track and as you do so glance over to the left, where across the fields the houses lining the path during its initial stages become visible. Further up, the track changes to a concrete surface. Continue to the crest of Portsdown Hill. On reaching the A333 you have a choice. Opposite you is the viewpoint car park where the walk began. Alternatively, if time permits, you may wish to head west along the grass verge beside the main road as far as Fort Widley. It is only a short distance from the end of the walk and adjacent to it is the starting point for the Fort Widley trail which you might like to try.

From the access point to the trail return to the viewpoint car park by the same route.

Historical Notes

Portsmouth: A key seafaring city and naval port since early times. Richard I was responsible for establishing a settlement on Portsea Island and it was he who built the first dock at Portsmouth in the late 12th century. The Tudor kings, Henry VII and Henry VIII, later constructed the first dry dock in the world here.

From its early beginnings Portsmouth evolved over the years into the south of England's largest and most important naval base. The city, where Charles Dickens was born, was heavily bombed during the Second World War.

There is much to see and do in Portsmouth with guided tours and museums among other attractions. HMS Victory and the Mary Rose are, of course, a major highlight of any visit to this city.

Forest of Bere: The ancient forest once covered a band of countryside from Southampton to the Sussex border. In the 11th century it was made a Royal Forest by William the Conqueror but little remains of it today apart from occasional patches of woodland. Much of the forest was cleared to provide oak timber for the building of Tudor warships.

Southwick: The village includes the headquarters of HMS Dryad, the Navy's School of Maritime Operations. At Southwick House, now virtually engulfed by the buildings of the naval establishment, the final preparations were made for the planned invasion of Europe on 6th June, 1944 − more commonly known as D-Day − and it was at Southwick House that Supreme Commander General Dwight Eisenhower and the Chiefs of Staff gathered to mastermind the huge operation. The operation room with its board used to plot the progress of Operation Overlord is still intact at Southwick and can be seen by obtaining special permission.

Portsdown Hill: The hill is 7 miles long, stretching from Bedhampton to Fareham. At the western end of the hill stands the Nelson Monument, a local landmark. Apart from its importance in terms of fortification, Portsdown Hill was also a vital link in communication, enabling signals to be transmitted between Whitehall and the fleet at Portsmouth.

Fort Widley: During the 1860s, the Prime Minister, Lord Palmerston, believing that the south coast of England might be under threat of attack by Napoleon III, authorised work to begin on building a line of forts on top of Portsdown Hill for the purpose of defending Spithead. Thankfully, they were never required for an active role. The low position of the forts and the way they so easily blended into the contours of the hill meant that from the north they were hardly visible at all. This was a deliberate ploy to deceive enemy forces should the French come ashore further along the coast in Sussex and then attempt to make an assault on Portsmouth from the rear. For anyone walking or driving along the ridge of Portsdown Hill the forts are easily seen at intervals of 1 to 1½ miles.

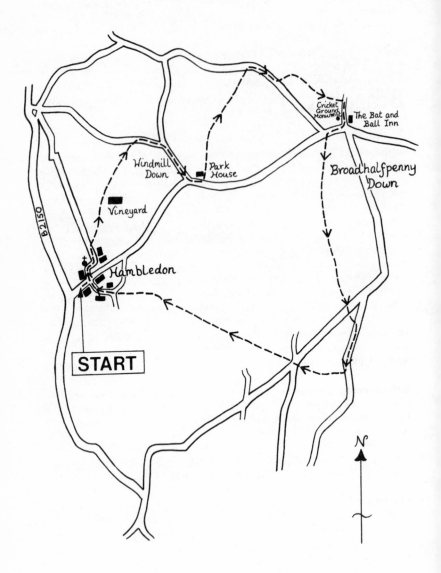

Cricket Ground
Monument

The Bat and
Ball Inn

Broadhalfpenny
Down

Windmill
Down

Park
House

Vineyard

B2150

Hambledon

START

N

Hambledon and Broadhalfpenny Down

Introduction: The walk begins in the lovely village of Hambledon, renowned as the 'cradle of cricket'. The village is set in excellent walking country, a fine mixture of high unspoilt chalk downland and thick beech woods. The route of this walk is designed to follow the contours of this spectacular landscape. From Hambledon it explores the agricultural heartland of Hampshire, crossing the wide fields and country paths to reach Broadhalfpenny Down where a welcome inn, The Bat and Ball, occupies a convenient if solitary position. The down here is, of course, famous for its crucial part in the early history of cricket.

The return includes some short, fairly dramatic climbs though there are rewarding views towards the coast at Portsmouth and to the east over the Sussex Downs, while in the west, on a good day, the outline of Fawley oil refinery can be seen on the edge of Southampton Water.

Distance: This is quite a long walk of about 7½ miles probably taking three hours or more to complete but the effort is well worth it. Maps: Ordnance Survey Landranger 185 and 196.

Refreshments: Hambledon has several inns including The Vine and The George Hotel. An extensive choice of food is available. The Bat and Ball at Broadhalfpenny Down serves bar food and has an a la carte restaurant and a beer garden.

How to get there: Follow the A32 and then take the B2150 Denmead – Waterlooville road to Hambledon. There is parking in the main street.

The Walk: Begin in the centre of Hambledon in the vicinity of the New Inn. Walk in an easterly direction along the main street and when you reach the post office cross over and head up the street opposite. Either side of you are rows of very pretty cottages and period houses. When, further up, you reach the entrance to the church, follow the road round to the right and then to the left.

Beyond this second bend there are very good views of the church over on the left. Turn right onto a waymarked footpath beside Hambledon County First School. From here there are splendid views back across Hambledon to the beech hangers beyond. Follow the path alongside the school yard. On the right here a charming tile-roofed dovecote is visible.

Walk along to the end of the school yard and then swing left and head up a track at the side of the school. When the track veers left into the school yard, swing diagonally right onto a thin path running through a corn field. Glancing back at this point there is a good view of the church tower between the trees. Proceed across to the far corner where there is a fence on the right beyond which is Hambledon Vineyard. Continue in the same direction heading out over Windmill Down. When, after a few moments, you reach the boundary between several fields proceed ahead keeping a hedge on the right. There are glorious views all around you from this high breezy ground; scenic wooded hills, rolling fields and spectacular downland stretching to the horizon.

Continue down the field edge, descending gradually to the road. Hambledon cricket ground is visible on the right as you drop down the slope. When you reach the stile in the field corner cross out to the road and turn right. Pass a turning on the left signposted to Chidden. Opposite the turning there is a footpath running across the fields back to the outskirts of Hambledon. Continue along the road following the sign to Clanfield (3 miles). Proceed up the slope and pass the entrance to the cricket club on the left. There is a path running alongside the club entrance and another on the opposite side of the road. Ignore both paths and keep on the road, dropping down towards Park House nestling amidst the trees. Note a farm over to the right across the fields.

On reaching the road junction bear left and follow the road signposted Clanfield and East Meon. Almost at once you pass Park House with its elegant brick and flint facade on the left. Immediately beyond the house turn left onto a waymarked path and after a few yards go through a gap at the side of the gate and continue along the track with a brick and flint wall on the right. The track follows one of the Wayfarer's Walk's circular routes now and here the path is quite grassy and somewhat overgown in places. Proceed ahead along the edge of the field. Pass through a smattering of trees and continue along the right hand boundary of the next field — the track having narrowed now to a rough path.

When you reach the field corner continue ahead into the trees, still on the grassy path. The way cuts through woodland between verges of brambles, nettles and scrub. After several minutes or so begin to look for a WW waymarker (Wayfarer's Walk); the logo is in black against a white background and can usually be found on tree trunks. Beside this one which is on the right of the path is a small post and arrow pointing left.

Take the left path and follow it through the trees over a patch of ground that is unexpectedly free of vegetation. Pass over a dilapidated old stile and emerge from the trees on the edge of a field. Veer half right and cross the field aiming for a waymarker in the far hedgerow which is not obvious at first. Gradually the position of the waymarker becomes apparent. Go through the gap in the boundary, negotiate a broken-down stile and then head straight out across the middle of the corn field following the narrow path between the crops, its outline indistinct at times.

When you reach the far boundary cross a stile out into the road. Turn right and head along the quiet country lane between the hedgerows. Soon the glorious semi-wooded slopes of Broadhalfpenny Down become visible over towards the horizon. After about ¼ mile a footpath sign comes into view on the right. Bear left opposite the sign onto a waymarked path running straight across the field. (The sign may be hidden from view if the hedge here has not been trimmed recently.)

On reaching the next field boundary cross the stile and then turn right, keeping to the right hand edge of the field. As you descend the slope glance over to the left and peeping between the trees on the distant horizon can be seen the sprawling outline of HMS Mercury, a naval shore establishment.

Nearer to hand, adjacent to the trees, are the buildings of a farm. Down in the field corner cross the stile and continue ahead along the right hand boundary. Up on the ridge of the adjoining field, to the left of a line of trees, the rooftop of The Bat and Ball inn nudges into view. Follow the gentle slope up to the top of the field, glancing back on occasions over a delightful, classically English scene of farmland and woods.

In the field corner go through a gate and out into the road. Bear right and on your left through a gap in the hedge there are spectacular glimpses of the western extremity of the South Downs of Sussex rising above Stoneridge Farm nestling in the foreground. Walk along the road, still with views of the downland ridge on your left. After a few yards you arrive at the entrance to the historic cricket ground on Broadhalfpenny Down on your right with The Bat and Ball opposite. Close to the road is the stone memorial bearing the following inscription: 'This stone marks the site of the ground of the Hambledon Cricket Club circa 1750-1787'.

From the memorial go to the road junction and bear right, signposted Hambledon and Fareham. Follow the road along the straight with light woodland on your right. When you reach a turning on the right signposted Chidden turn left over a stile in the opposite hedgerow. From the footpath sign you will see there are two parallel routes heading up the steep hillside in front of you. Take the right hand path and climb up the slope to the stile in the field boundary. Glancing back now you are treated to delightful views of the cricket ground and the earlier route of the walk where it cuts across a rippling rural landscape of fields, woods and downland.

Cross the stile and swing right following a track running over the high ground of Broadhalfpenny Down towards the trees. Looking at the view a little more closely you can easily identify some of the landmarks encountered during the outward leg of the walk; the approach to The Bat and Ball through the fields and the farm buildings spotted just before the climb up to the road by the inn.

Soon the view on the right is obscured by a burst of woodland immediately alongside the track. Continue ahead between the trees and undergrowth. After some minutes the track curves left and now it is enclosed by a thin belt of trees and bushes. In one of the openings on the left there are superb views stretching to the south coast and on a good day you can glimpse Portsmouth, Langstone Harbour and the dark blue ribbon of the Solent merging with the horizon. Looking to the east here you can just spot the windmill near Chalton over on the skyline.

Proceed down the track until you reach Scotland Cottage on the left. Immediately beyond the cottage join a waymarked path running into the trees. Follow the path cutting through a narrow belt of trees and undergrowth until it becomes overgrown and virtually impassable in places. When it does, step into the field on the left and walk along its edge until further down you reach a gap on the right. Pass through it at the point where the original path joins a track and continue ahead following the track down between fields. Soon it reaches a field and peters out just inside the boundary. Proceed ahead across the field towards a hedgerow on the far side. A hill rises steeply above the boundary and there are several dwellings clearly visible just below the ridge.

Drop down gently to the hedge using a smattering of trees as a useful landmark. Look for a stile and waymarker amongst the trees. Cross the stile and then take the waymarked path on the other side of the track. Bear left for a few yards in the field and then head uphill to a stile in the hedgerow — the first of a series of stiles to be found at regular intervals on this stretch of the walk. You have been warned!

There are good rearward views as you make the climb up the field slope. Cross all the stiles along the left boundary, noting a detached house on the right, and eventually you reach the road. Turn right and pass the entrance to Harrowgate House and Down House adjacent to it. Follow the lane uphill cutting between high hedgerows. Soon it levels out. Pass a turning on the left and just beyond Old Mill House on the right bear right onto a footpath signposted Hambledon.

Follow the path between fences and after about 50 yards cross a stile and continue out across the field. On the distant horizon, visibility permitting, you can spot the chimneys of Fawley oil refinery. In the gap in the next boundary cross the stile and proceed ahead. Aim for the opening in the next boundary and then drop down the steep slope veering slightly right and making for the field exit in the far boundary. A number of converging tracks are visible just beyond the distant fence.

If there is an electric fence in this field to protect grazing sheep then follow the perimeter of the field. When you leave the field ignore all the various tracks and continue ahead on a narrow path across another field. Follow the path through the field and up the slope. All around you are open fields and downland expanses. There is a sense of isolation about this stretch of the walk as if any form of civilization is a long way from your route.

When you reach a waymarker and a stony cross track proceed ahead now following the right edge of the next field. Keep on this path beside a burst of woodland and descend steeply into a sudden hidden fold. Rise sharply the other side heading for the trees in front of you. Follow the main path into the wood but soon you emerge the other side for it is only a brief association with the trees. Continue along a narrow path between the now familiar crops with an area of extensive woodland over on the left. When you reach a track at the end of the trees cross over and follow another narrow path between rows of corn.

On reaching a stile in the field boundary cross it and turn left along a wide grassy ride. Note the buildings of Rushmere stud on the right and once past the house look for a stile in the right hand fence. Negotiate the stile and then walk ahead for a few yards onto a drive and bear left. There is a waymarked path on the right here but at the time of writing, the path was particularly overgrown and unless it has been cleared of undergrowth I recommend you take the main drive between paddocks to the road and turn right; at the fork swing left. If the path is passable follow it to the road and bear right and then left at the fork.

Drop down steeply into Hambledon between rows of picturesque cottages and graceful period houses. Further down you pass the entrance to Speltham Down owned by the National Trust. Follow the road round and past Hill House. Proceed to the junction in the centre of the village.

Historical Notes

Hambledon: The Bishop of Winchester granted a weekly market here in the 13th century and looking at it today, a quiet village of pretty Georgian and timber-framed houses lying in a peaceful valley in the heart of rural Hampshire, it is hard to believe that it was once a prosperous, fast-growing town with a church which was enlarged several times. The church was later restored in the 19th century.

Hambledon Vineyard: With soil not dissimilar to the Champagne region of France, Hambledon is one of the largest vineyards in the country with its vines yielding 8,000 to 10,000 bottles of white wine a year. The vineyard which comprises five acres on Windmill Down was established in the early 1950s by Major General Sir Guy Salisbury-Jones, a distinguished soldier who fought in the First World War and who later became Marshal of the Diplomatic Corps. It was suggested to him one day that the sunny south facing slopes adjoining his Hambledon home would be most suitable as a vineyard. After a visit to Burgundy to seek the advice of experts in the field, Sir Guy returned home having acquired 4,000 vines during his trip. At last the suggestion had turned to reality!

Broadhalfpenny Down: James I granted the Bishop of Winchester the right to hold fairs in Hambledon early in the 17th century and the toll paid to the lord of the manor for setting up the booths was a broad halfpenny. The stretch of downland 2 miles north east of Hambledon thus became known as Broadhalfpenny Down. The down is the site of the famous and historic cricket ground where the Hambledon Cricket Club played. Originally the game was played with two forked sticks as stumps. The club, established about 1750, was responsible for laying down the rules of the game as we know it today.

'Little Switzerland': Petersfield and Steep

Introduction: With its spectacular beech hangers, green hills and downland, the countryside of East Hampshire, known as 'Little Switzerland', boasts some of the most striking scenery in the county. Certainly the Edwardian poet Edward Thomas loved it dearly. He lived here for a time and was moved to write about the area in his work.

The route, which encompasses the best of this delightful scenery, begins in the country town of Petersfield – the imposing square in the town centre is worth closer investigation – and then immediately heads north to the sprawling village of Steep, aptly named because of its hilly position below the wooded escarpment. The walk follows a meandering route through attractive woodland and along quiet field paths and lanes to the top of Shoulder of Mutton Hill where, in a peaceful glade, there is a sarsen stone in memory of Edward Thomas. From here there are stunning views to the south between lines of lovely old beeches. Thankfully, the vistas have hardly changed since Thomas strolled here, savouring the special distinctive beauty of this corner of Hampshire.

The walk heads back via gentle paths to the outskirts of Steep where there is a conveniently placed inn and on across rolling farmland and parkland. This final leg into Petersfield offers a welcome alternative to the steep wooded stretches of earlier.

Distance: This is a walk of 7 miles and at a fairly gentle pace will probably take about three and a half hours. The outward leg is hilly in places. Map: Ordnance Survey Landranger 197.

Refreshments: The Harrow at Steep, about ½ mile from the route of the walk, is a delightfully unspoilt country inn with an inglenook fireplace, two small bars and real ale from the barrel. The Cricketers on the western edge of Steep also provides a varied menu.

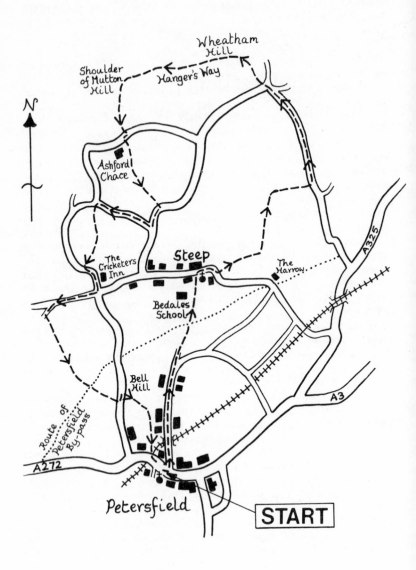

How to get there: The walk begins in the fee-paying car park in Park Road, Petersfield. It is just to the south of the A272 and a little to the east of the railway station.

The Walk: From the car park in the centre of Petersfield proceed to the junction (the exit prohibited to vehicles) and bear right into Chapel Street. At the junction go across into Tilmore Road and walk up the road and over the railway bridge. Further up the road there are splendid views of the town and the surrounding hills and downland. Butser Hill to the south rises to nearly 900 ft and marks the western extremity of the South Downs.

Continue up the road between the houses, passing Highfield Road on the right. Drop down the hill, ignoring the footpath on the left, and when the road curves right at Tilmore Gardens go forward onto a waymarked path with a stile just to the right of the entrance to Steep House Nursing and Residential Home. Note the plaque on the footpath sign which reads: 'Jack's post. Donated by Petersfield Ramblers Club in appreciation of Mr Jack Tully, a founder member, November 1st, 1986'.

Follow the path along the edge of the field of rough pasture and soon it curves left to a stile. Once over the stile continue in a northerly direction and in a few moments you reach the Petersfield bypass. (The bypass was still under construction when this book was written but it is scheduled to open in the autumn of 1992. Provision has been made for members of the public to cross it on foot.)

Walk over the bridge and then turn right, joining a path between fence and hedge. Soon the sprawling buildings of Bedales School come into view. Continue on the path and on the right there are glimpses of wooded hills in the distance. Pass through the trees and note the excellent views of Bedales and its spacious, well-tended grounds on the left.

The route of the walk is along the left hand side of Steep church close to the vestry extension added in 1989. Turn right on reaching Church Road and walk down to where it swings right. The Harrow pub is a ten minute walk down the road; the inn is on the left just before the bypass. On leaving the Harrow return to this bend, take the waymarked path into the woods and bear right at once following the path as it descends steeply through the dense, dark woodland. Soon the path reaches a stile and once over it head down to the farm buildings.

In the field corner cross the stile and then the boundary fence and follow the path running alongside the old buildings. There are glorious views of beech hangers on the left up towards Shoulder of Mutton Hill, Wheatham Hill and the middle stages of the walk. Further on, join a track at the entrance to a farm and after several yards turn left and follow another track. Pass over a stream under some trees and then, as the track swings right, continue ahead for a few yards up to a stile. Take the left hand route avoiding the path straight in front of you climbing up the bank. Keep on the main path through the woods. Walk across the garden of a detached house following the waymarker signs and continue into the woodland on the far side. Pass to the left of some buildings and at the end of them turn right onto a waymarked track.

Beyond the buildings avoid a turning on the right and a track on the left and continue past some garages and offices towards several gates with gaps at the side. Once through them follow the track out to the road. Turn left and pass a house called The Great Oast on the left and then a lodge on the right. The narrow lane begins to climb steeply now between wooded banks.

Further up the hill, the road forks. Keep left and when you reach the road junction after a few yards swing sharp right for a short distance and then look for a stile and a waymarked path in the left hand hedge. Cross the stile and walk up the right hand edge of the field. At the top, just before the next stile, pause for a few moments to admire the glorious views of rolling hills, woods and downland reaching to the horizon.

Pass over the stile into the woods and after a couple of yards swing left onto a wide, deeply rutted track running through the trees. The track, known as Hanger's Way, climbs steeply in places up towards the summit of Shoulder of Mutton Hill. The clay soil is quite slippery in places so do take care. Soon there are magnificent views on the left of Petersfield and the downs beyond. Eventually the track levels out between banks of undergrowth and wild flowers, bushes and occasional fallen trees.

Once the steep pull is behind you, begin to watch out for a path on the left descending sharply into the trees; a gate is visible a few yards further down the bank. Do not take this path, however, but use it instead as a landmark. Continue along Hanger's Way through the tunnel of trees and after several minutes you reach a track on the right. Pass this turning and proceed ahead. Soon you encounter a stile on the right and a sign for Hanger's Way. About 250 yards beyond the stile bear left onto a path also signposted Hanger's Way. Follow it between banks of undergrowth and soon you begin to descend the steep slope. This is the famous beauty spot known as Shoulder of Mutton Hill. Further down there are glorious unrivalled vistas opening out between the beech trees, surely one of the highlights of this very memorable walk. The views from here are predominantly of Steep and the countryside to the south of Petersfield.

Continue down the slope, seemingly almost vertical in places, and soon a distinctive sarsen stone comes into view just below. The plaque on the stone reads: 'This hillside is dedicated to the memory of Edward Thomas, poet, born in Lambeth 3rd March, 1878, killed in the Battle of Arras, 9th April, 1917'. Beneath the dates is the following inscription: 'And I rose up and knew that I was tired and continued my journey'. Just below the stone is a seat which provides weary walkers with the chance to pause and reflect and to admire the magnificent views.

Proceed down the hillside ignoring the path over to the right and continue on the main route, following it as it curves a little to the right down towards a large property known as Ashford Chace. Further down, look for a gap among the trees and descend a flight of steps beneath them. Cross a stile and walk along the right hand edge of the field. On reaching the road turn right for a few steps and then bear left over the stile onto a waymarked path. Follow the track and then just before it swings right join a narrow path running through the undergrowth. Pass over a bridge after several yards and then enter an area of pretty woodland. The path swings sharp right, continues through the trees and then bears left. Shortly you can hear the sound of rushing water and when you do so turn right onto another narrow path and go down to the road with the surprising yet delightful spectacle of a plunging waterfall on the right just before the junction.

Turn right on the bend in the road and walk up to the next right turning. Take the turning and after several minutes you pass the entrance to Garden Hill on the right. Proceed on up the road through the trees and when you reach a junction at the top of the hill swing left for a few yards, passing Island Farm, and then turn left onto a waymarked path cutting between trees and private gardens. Soon, there are impressive views over on the left of rolling open countryside stretching to the Sussex border and beyond. Glancing behind you there are glimpses still of the wooded escarpment of earlier.

Follow the path as it zig zags down through the trees to a stile. Cross over it and walk along the right hand boundary of the field keeping the trees on the right. The houses visible on this stretch of the walk form the outskirts of Steep. On reaching the next stile in the right hand hedge cross over on to a footpath and after several yards join a track by some private lock-up garages. At the road, cross over and continue on a narrow path between hedges as far as the main road.

Turn left and pass The Cricketers on the left. Immediately beyond it at the crossroads bear right and take the turning signposted Langrish. Pass the entrance to Collyers garden nursery on the left. Continue for a minute or two and then take the waymarked path on the left opposite the entrance to Stonerwood Park. Veer left for a short distance to the stile in the boundary. Join a path cutting between hedges and undergrowth. After a few steps cross the drive and make for the stile. Once over it follow the right hand edge of the field as far as the corner. Cross into the next field by means of yet another stile. Continue close to the right hand edge and then pass over the stile in the field corner. Walk beneath the trees for several yards and then take the stile into the next field.

Proceed along the left hand edge and in the corner, on reaching the route of the Petersfield bypass once again, turn right and follow the path along the top of the embankment until you reach the footbridge. Cross over to the opposite side and then veer left and proceed along the southern bank of the road. Keep on top of the embankment until you are level with the point at which you reached the bypass and then turn right over a stile. Follow the right hand edge of the field until you reach a stile and a gate. Cross it and join a track. Continue ahead along the track until you reach the road.

Bear left here, walk along the pavement for a few yards and then cross over and turn right on to Bell Hill Ridge. Proceed along the tarmac drive between detached houses and at the end of the drive continue ahead to join a narrow path with rolling fields on the left.

When you reach the entrance to Greenfields on the left, turn right under the trees and then, after a few yards, bear left at the fork. Follow the path between hedges and fences. Pass some allotments on the left and proceed ahead. Further on, the way broadens out to a wide tarmac path. When, shortly, you arrive at the main road turn left, go over the level crossing and on reaching Chapel Street bear right and return to the car park in Park Road where the walk started.

Historical Notes

Petersfield: The focal point of this charming 18th century town, once a prosperous centre for the wool trade, is the large square in which stands the statue of William III, depicted on horseback and dressed, absurdly, as a Roman. The statue, erected in 1753, was restored early in the 20th century. The town became well known during the coaching era and at one time there were as many as nine inns here.

The restored parish church dates from the 12th century and is situated near the statue of King William. One of the headstones here is in memory of John Small who died in 1826. He was one of the pioneering Hambledon cricketers and his epitaph reads:

> 'Praises on Tombs are Trifles Vainly Spent
> A Man's Good Name is His Own Monument'

Bedales School: One of Britain's most famous public school institutions, Bedales was founded by John Haden Badley. He died aged 102 in 1967. Badley as a headmaster was a man of great vision and far from conventional. His ideas on education and discipline were quite revolutionary and he was sometimes regarded as a controversial figure by his more traditionalist peers.

Steep church: The partly Norman church of All Saints includes a Victorian bell turret, a lychgate and several memorials including one to Basil Marden who was killed in an avalanche in the Andes in 1928. There is a memorial window, too, dedicated to the poet Edward Thomas and designed and engraved by Laurence Whistler. The window was dedicated in 1978, the centenary of Thomas's birth.

Shoulder of Mutton Hill: The hill bears a prehistoric sarsen stone on its higher grassy slopes which is a memorial to the Edwardian poet Edward Thomas who was killed in the First World War.

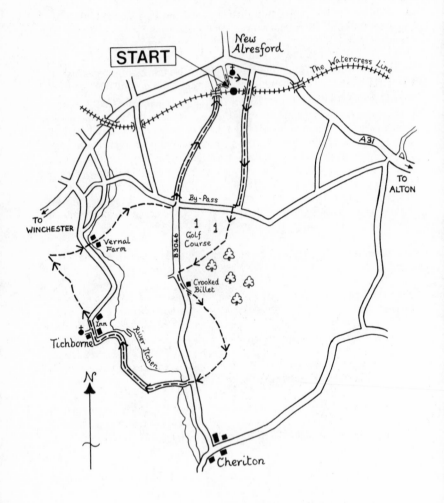

New Alresford and Tichborne

Introduction: The walk begins in New Alresford, a delightful Georgian town with many handsome buildings lining its streets and the attraction of the enthusiastically supported Mid-Hants Railway 'Watercress Line'. For those who mourn the passing of steam travel, here is the chance to recapture some of its magical flavour on a ten mile journey beginning at New Alresford station. This is also the starting point for our walk. One of its most interesting features is Tichborne, a sprawling village in the unspoilt Itchen valley that boasts many thatched cottages and an intriguing tale dating back to the 12th century of what is known as 'The Tichborne Dole'. Part of the route coincides with the Wayfarer's Walk.

Distance: The walk is about 5½ miles and should take two to two and a half hours to complete. Map: Ordnance Survey Landranger 185.

Refreshments: New Alresford has a good selection of hotels and public houses. The Swan Hotel serves bar food, afternoon teas and also has a restaurant. The Bell Hotel opposite has a good choice of bar food as well as a restaurant. The Old School House in West Street has a restaurant and a tea room. The Tichborne Arms, a little over halfway round the circuit, is a charming thatched pub which serves bar snacks. The Cricketers Arms is almost at the end of the walk and provides bar food.

How to get there: New Alresford is about 7 miles east of Winchester and 14 miles south of Basingstoke on the A31. The walk begins in the car park beside the station at the end of Station Road which is a turning off West Street. There is a fee for parking.

The Walk: From the car park in New Alresford walk away from the direction of the Mid-Hants Railway Watercress Line and along Station Road. After a few yards you reach a public footpath on the right between the police station and the churchyard.

Take the path and follow it until you reach a junction with a wall immediately in front of you. Turn right here and keep to the path with the churchyard on your right and houses and a hedgerow on your left. Follow the path until you reach a road. Turn right here and immediately pass over the Watercress Line. There is an excellent view of the station from the bridge. Proceed ahead along the road, passing some houses and then a school on the right. Press on down the hill and go round to the right beside some very pretty white cottages. After a few yards cross the road and walk onto a path running up over the bypass.

Follow the path, signposted Cheriton, towards the golf course. Keep on the path as it veers right over the fairways following the various arrows and waymarker posts. Beware of golf balls! In the adjacent field proceed up the slope by keeping close to the left boundary hedge. There are good views of New Alresford over to the right as you make the ascent. At the top of the slope the path enters an area of unspoilt woodland.

Keep to the path as it gradually descends between lines of trees with frequent vistas offering glimpses of rolling countryside. After several minutes you reach a gate and the road is just a couple of yards beyond it. Turn left opposite a private road to Tichborne Park and follow the B3046 for several hundred yards. There is no pavement on this stretch of road so take care and if necessary, for safety's sake, keep in single file. Immediately beyond a cottage, Crooked Billet, turn left onto a waymarked footpath, part of the Wayfarer's Walk. Follow the track for a few yards and then join a narrow path running between hedges to the left of a corrugated barn. Soon the hedgerow on the right gives way to reveal very attractive farmland views and wooded hills in the distance. In a few moments you enter a tunnel of trees, cool and pleasantly shaded in high summer. Climb a gentle slope and further on the trees and bushes give way to good open views. Turn right as per the waymarker post and follow a path sloping down to the road between fields and hedgerows choked with wild flowers and undergrowth. There are farm buildings and occasional dwellings down below in the valley.

When you reach the B3046 cross over and take the lane opposite (signposted Tichborne). Pass over the clear fast-flowing waters of a stream and then leave the Wayfarer's Walk as it heads left away from the road. Keep on the lane and soon you reach Tichborne. The road winds its way through the delightful village. On the right is the river Itchen which has its source near here. Shortly you reach the turning to St Andrew's church on the left.

Continue through the village and soon you reach a sharp right hand bend in the road. Here you will see a track with a footpath sign in front of you running to the left of an attractive cottage. If you fancy some refreshment at this stage then turn right and follow the road for about 100 yards until you reach The Tichborne Arms. To continue the walk proceed along the track (avoiding a path on the left after a few yards) and follow it as it cuts through some undulating farmland. Avoid a waymarked path on the right and a turning on the left. There are glorious views behind you over the village and beyond. The church tower at Tichborne can be seen nestling amid the trees. In the top right corner of the field bear right and continue along the right hand edge of the next field.

Walk down through the fields to the road by keeping to the right hand edge. There are some very pretty pastoral views of the Hampshire countryside from these fields, as well as glimpses of the meandering Itchen.

When you reach the road go straight across and along the track that leads to Vernal Farm. Walk between the house on the right and the farm buildings on the left and continue ahead. After a few yards you pass some houses this time on the left. The track narrows to become a path slicing through the fields. Follow the path and after about five minutes you find yourself walking alongside a fence on the left − with the Alresford and Bishops Sutton bypass down below the embankment. On reaching the road bridge bear left and follow the road back to New Alresford passing The Cricketers Arms on the right. At length you pass beneath the railway bridge carrying the Watercress Line. If you wish to return immediately to the point at which the walk began and thus avoid New Alresford town centre, turn right beyond the bridge and the access road will lead you back to the station car park.

Historical Notes

New Alresford: The name 'New Alresford' suggests the town is modern but there is nothing very new about it at all. Before the Conquest it was in the possession of the Bishops of Winchester. In the 12th century it was extensively rebuilt by Bishop de Lucy. It prospered − so much so that it was later to be considered one of our most important wool markets. In 1644 the Royalists set the town alight following the battle of Cheriton nearby. In 1689 most of the town was again burned to the ground when another fire swept hungrily through it. As a result, very few houses seen in the town today were built before the 17th century. An impressive feature of New Alresford is the medieval bridge at the bottom of Broad Street. Also, at a house in Broad Street, novelist Mary Russell Mitford, author of 'Our Village', was born.

The Watercress Line: The Mid-Hants 'Watercress Line' is privately run by volunteers. It was officially opened on 30th April 1977, a long awaited but well deserved reward for its group of enthusiastic supporters. At that time the service terminated at Ropley, 3 miles away, but these days it is 10 miles in length, running from Alresford to Alton. The original line was 17 miles long and ran between Alton and Winchester. With its gradients, cuttings and embankments the line came to be regarded as an engineering masterpiece. At

Medstead and Four Marks it climbs to the highest point on the route, known by locals as 'going over the alps'. In its day the line provided a vital link for the local watercress industry — hence the name 'Watercress Line' — supplying much of the rest of the country.

Several of the steam locomotives are typical of those one would have expected to find anywhere in the country during the last 60 years or so.

For information regarding train services you can ring the talking timetable on 0962 734866. There is a link with British Rail services at Alton.

Tichborne: The village is famous for the story of 'The Tichborne Dole'. In 1150 Lady Mabella Tichborne, wife of Sir Roger Tichborne, requested her husband to form a charity to help the poor people of the parish. Sir Roger, a man not known for his compassion, agreed to provide sick and needy parishioners with a 'dole' of bread annually on 25th March — Lady Day. However, there was one condition. Sir Roger would only leave to charity the corn in the fields around which his sick and dying wife could crawl in the time it took for a firebrand to burn. Much to his amazement Lady Mabella rose from her deathbed and crawled around 23 acres of land before the fire died. To this day the villagers of Tichborne and Cheriton still receive a gallon of flour each and half a gallon for children.

Six centuries after the tradition of the dole was originated the Tichborne name was at the centre of a much publicised trial when a man claiming to be Roger Tichborne, the heir to the estate, turned up two years after the real Tichborne had disappeared while on his way to Australia. However, the court found the man guilty of fraud and he was eventually sentenced to 14 years' penal servitude.

St Andrew's church at Tichborne is a most interesting building in a delightful spot. It is pre-Conquest with 12th century aisles. The chancel is 11th century and the communion rail and the lovely high box-pews are Jacobean.

Selborne

Introduction: Selborne is famous as the home of the celebrated 18th century naturalist Gilbert White. His book 'The Natural History of Selborne' is still available in several editions and it brings many visitors to the village every year. With good reason. In the words of the National Trust guide 'the area is the mecca of naturalists and nature lovers, the living green outdoor laboratory of Gilbert White'.

The route of the walk takes you right through the heart of the area he loved so much and includes the famous Selborne Hanger, a beautiful tree-clad hill stretched out like a slumbering giant above the village, before heading across country to the church at Newton Valence. The return leg is a delightful stroll through the trees on Selborne Common.

Distance: The walk is about 5 miles in length. Allow about two hours to undertake it. Map: Ordnance Survey Landranger 186.

Refreshments: The Queen's Hotel and The Selborne Arms are the two inns on this walk. Both are in Selborne itself and both serve food. Bush House next to The Selborne Arms provides coffee, luncheons and cream teas. There are a number of pubs in the locality including The Royal Oak at Lower Farringdon though none of them will be found on the actual route of this walk.

How to get there: Selborne is about 4 miles south of Alton on the B3006. There is a free car park behind The Selborne Arms where the walk officially begins.

The Walk: From the car park in Selborne follow the sign to the Zig Zag path and when you reach its foot climb it to the top of Selborne Hanger, where there are some splendid views across Hampshire through a leafy curtain of trees. The Zig Zag path was created by Gilbert White and his brother who cut it in 1753. It was intended as a short cut to the top of the Hanger. The path enables thousands of people to visit this beautiful spot every year and to do so by a clever and novel means. There is a seat at the top of the Zig Zag path where one can pause to rest and admire the scene.

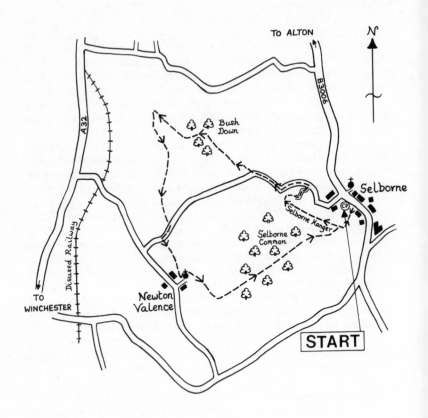

From the seat go to the wishing stone a few yards away and then take the short flight of steps onto a path. Follow the path in a westerly direction along the edge of the hillside with grand views of Selborne down below you on the right. Avoid all turnings. This is a particularly beautiful stretch of the walk as it passes beneath a thick canopy of lovely old beech trees with glimpses of the village at regular intervals.

After some time you emerge from the trees at a junction with a bank and a hedge immediately in front of you at the foot of the hill. Turn right at the junction and follow a path between the fields. The path bends sharply several times before arriving at a road beside an attractive house known as 'Fisher's Lodge'. Turn left at the road and follow it for nearly ½ mile. The road bends a couple of times and passes through a tunnel of trees. When you are clear of the trees and at a point where the road turns left, walk ahead onto a track flanked by fields. After a few yards there is a gate with a bridleway sign beside it on the left. Pass through the gate and then walk diagonally right across the field towards another gate in the trees. On reaching it pass through to the stile and then walk diagonally left and uphill towards more trees. Go to the right of a solitary tree in the field and then, as you approach the woodland, watch for a gateway leading you into it. Join a clearly defined track and proceed ahead; the track can be very muddy in places. When at last you are clear of the woodland continue ahead on a path cutting through farmland with glimpses of soft pretty countryside in the distance.

Follow the route beneath a line of electricity pylons and then continue to the next row of pylons. The path is lined by high hedges at this point. Just beyond the second line of pylons look out for a waymarked path running diagonally across the field on the left.

Take the path across the field passing beneath the pylons. Over on the right there are good views across to Pelham Place and Newton Common on the far side of the A32. Descend the slope to the stile in the field corner. Once over it bear left and then cross a second stile into the next field. Follow the field edge down the slope, keeping to it as it curves broadly round to the right and up the other side towards the pylons and the trees.

When you reach the footpath sign pointing the way you have just come, turn right and drop down the bank to a stile. Cross over and descend the slope by following the track, keeping to the right hand boundary of the field. There are good views on this stretch over a wide band of countryside. After nearly ½ mile you arrive at the road. Turn right and pass Reed Cottage on the left. A few yards beyond it you come upon an intriguing octagonal-shaped lodge on the left. Cross the stile beside it and then the next stile almost immediately and continue ahead up through the fields. The surroundings here assume the appearance of private parkland with clusters of trees and grazing cattle. Further up there are good views of Newton Valence Place over on the left. In the top right hand corner of the field go through the wrought-iron gate and out into the drive to Newton Valence Place. Cross over and pass through the gate opposite.

Proceed half right across the field towards some trees and a house. Go through a wooden gate and follow the path with a laurel hedge on the left. On reaching the next drive bear left towards the lychgate of St Mary's church, Newton Valence. (To visit the village turn right on reaching the drive.)

At the churchyard take the path running to the left of the church. The path cuts through a splendid avenue of yew trees and then enters a copse. Cross a stile on the far side of the trees and bear right following the field edge. The large house next to the church can be seen on the right now. Aim for the stile in the next boundary up ahead and then once over it go slightly right towards the stile in the distant trees. Negotiate the stile and follow the path into the woodland. You are now on the edge of Selborne Common which is in the care of the National Trust. During the 19th century cricket was played here and cattle once grazed among the trees and the grassy glades. Go forward for a few yards to reach a major junction of paths.

Proceed ahead on the path marked 'Selborne – via Church Path'. The path is delightful, meandering between tall beeches and banks of undergrowth. When at length you reach a junction turn right and after some moments you arrive back at the top of the Zig Zag path. Descend the path to the car park and if there is time a visit to Selborne's St Mary's church is worthwhile.

Historical Notes

Gilbert White: The famous naturalist was born in 1720. He was an extremely gifted man and in his time he was a curate, a naturalist and an Oxford don. His father was a barrister and his grandfather vicar of the parish. After school he went to Oxford and became a Fellow and Dean of Oriel but he returned to his beloved Selborne and became curate there.

He made his home at The Wakes which is now a most interesting museum devoted to the memory of its former owner. Selborne is and always has been a must for naturalists. There are a number of different editions of Gilbert White's classic 'The Natural History of Selborne'. It has been translated into French, Danish, Swedish and Japanese and was first published in 1788 five years before his death. His original manuscript was sold at Christie's in June 1980 for £100,000.

The Wakes Museum is well worth a visit if time allows. The house was bought by R.W.Oates and the Oates Museum in the house illustrates the story of naturalist and explorer Francis Oates and his nephew Captain Lawrence Oates who joined the fateful Antarctic expedition in 1911. The Wakes Museum is open from Wednesday to Sunday 11 am–5 pm between March and October.

St Mary's church, Newton Valence: The Early English church was restored in 1871. There is a 13th century piscina in the side chapel and the chancel is 13th century also. The magnificent yew standing in the churchyard is about seven yards round. Gilbert White was curate here for a time.

St Mary's church, Selborne: In the church there are reminders of Gilbert White including a window dedicated to him depicting St Francis of Assisi feeding the birds. The window has 64 birds in it. St Mary's is about seven centuries old but the site for the original church was given by the wife of Edward the Confessor. It has Norman arcades and a 16th century Flemish triptych over the altar given to the church by Gilbert White's brother. There is also a chapel with a flight of steps dating back 700 years, which originally had pews on them designed for children. Now they have coffin stones which were removed here from a priory. As at Newton Valence there is a wonderful old yew tree in the churchyard.

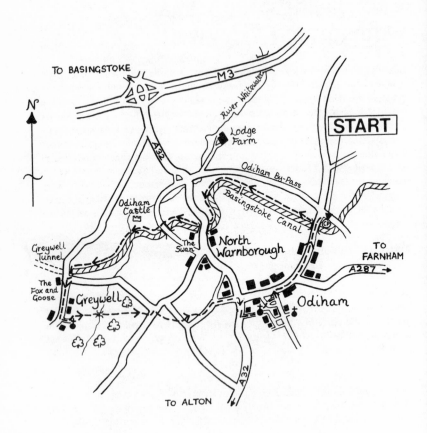

The Basingstoke Canal: Odiham and Greywell

Introduction: The walk begins near Odiham. With its wide main street lined with a variety of handsome 18th century buildings, it is without doubt a jewel among the smaller towns of southern England. The route then follows for some considerable time the sleepy waters of the restored Basingstoke Canal, passing through some very pretty Hampshire countryside. Although long since fallen into commercial disuse its soul has been revived at last thanks to a joint project undertaken by the Surrey and Hampshire councils to transform it into a leisure amenity. A much sadder landmark on the walk is Odiham's ruined castle standing on the banks of the canal; only the picturesque 13th century keep remains of the place from where King John set out to sign the Magna Carta. Further on is the delightful village of Greywell with a disused tunnel on the canal, one of the longest in southern England.

Distance: The walk is about 4 miles and should take about two hours. Map: Ordnance Survey Landranger 186.

Refreshments: There are some excellent inns on the route of this walk and several have gardens which are particularly worth a visit during the warmer months of the year. The Waterwitch and The Swan both serve bar snacks. The Kings Arms Hotel and The George Hotel in Odiham provide bar snacks and both have restaurants as well. The Fox and Goose at Greywell offers bar food. All have good beer!

How to get there: Odiham is about 6 miles east of Basingstoke near junction 5 of the M3. From the main street take the road signposted 'The Waterwitch' and proceed to the Odiham Wharf car park at the bottom. The walk begins here.

The Walk: From the car park head in a general westerly direction towards the road bridge over the Basingstoke Canal. On reaching the towpath pass under Colt Hill Bridge, c 1792. Continue along the towpath with gardens of the Waterwitch inn on the opposite bank. Walk ahead with the canal hard on your left and the Odiham bypass across the fields on your right. Keep on the towpath and after nearly a mile you reach a narrow bridge spanning the canal.

Continue ahead along the towpath following the canal as it begins a gradual left hand curve towards the houses of Odiham's neighbouring village North Warnborough; the canal snakes its way round the village. When you reach a brick road bridge, continue ahead – the dank, cold tunnel echoing the muffled rumble of traffic above. Immediately beyond the bridge a flight of steps on the right will lead you up onto the road, beside which is The Swan public house. To continue the walk proceed ahead and follow the canal as it swings round to the left and approaches a swing road bridge ahead. Pass a row of cottages on the right, cross over the road and press on along the towpath.

Shortly you reach the entrance to Odiham Castle a few yards from the canal on the right. After a visit to the castle return to the towpath and turn right. In a few moments you pass over the river Whitewater which crosses the canal and then the countryside on your right begins to open out a little. Soon the path rises above the level of the water and now you are approaching Greywell tunnel.

When you reach the entrance it is possible to get a closer look at it by negotiating a winding, somewhat precipitous flight of steps which leads you down to the mouth of the tunnel. Returning to the towpath turn left and then left again. Now you are walking above the entrance to the tunnel. The path narrows and cuts between the gardens of houses before it reaches a stile leading you into the road. Turn right and then when you reach the junction after a few yards turn left. On the opposite side of the road is The Fox and Goose. Proceed along the road passing the houses of Greywell as you do so.

Greywell, voted Hampshire's best kept village in 1971, is surely one of the prettiest in the county. It is a peaceful little place with a collection of most attractive houses and cottages to enhance it. One property which particularly stands out is a large rambling brick and timber house on the right hand side of the road. Shortly you reach a gate and a path flanked by hedging and fencing on your left which takes you to the church of St Mary the Virgin. Take the path to visit the church and then as you leave it head for a kissing gate clearly visible ahead of you, taking you into a field adjoining the churchyard. Walk diagonally across the field and, not quite in the far corner, make for a stile leading onto a tree-shaded path.

Negotiate the stile and then cross over the river Whitewater once again, this time by means of a concrete footbridge. Follow the path as it cuts between trees and undergrowth. After a few yards you reach a stile in a rustic wooden fence. Cross over it and walk ahead. The path opens out now as it crosses a narrow field. Head towards a double stile in front of you and cross into the next field. Cross this field by walking diagonally left or – if the crops make the going difficult — skirt it by the left hand edge until you reach another stile taking you into the road.

On reaching the road turn left and walk along it for a few yards until you come to a stile and a footpath sign on your right. Climb the stile and then, after a couple of yards, you will see another stile in the hedgerow. Negotiate the stile and then walk diagonally right across the field and into the corner. There you will find another stile. Pass over it into the next field and then go across it to arrive at a stile which enables you to pass into the road.

Cross the road to reach a stile and accompanying footpath sign. Cross the stile and then walk half right across the field towards a stile in the far hedgerow. On reaching it cross onto a narrow path which skirts the edge of some school buildings. Turn right, walk along the path passing the school buildings as you do so, and moments later you reach the road. Turn left and walk along it. You are now back on the outskirts of Odiham.

When the road bends left turn into West Street and follow it between rows of cottages to the road junction. Then turn right and immediately after The Crown public house on your left is a narrow lane bordered by a high wall on the left and a field on the right. This will bring you to Odiham's parish church of All Saints. Turn left when you reach the church and then walk down into a most charming and elegant square lined with some very attractive houses and cottages. Opposite you is The Bell. This is a most enchanting part of Odiham, quaint and largely undiscovered by the passing motorist and traveller. This area is called The Bury. Turn right and take the road to the right of a property called 'Little Court'. Shortly you reach Mayhill County Junior School on the right. Turn left opposite the entrance beside some pretty cottages on the corner.

Follow the road to the junction and then turn left and walk along the road until you arrive in the main street of Odiham. Turn right and then take the road signposted 'The Waterwitch'. Pass the inn and then continue on the road as far as the Odiham Wharf car park where the walk began.

Historical Notes

The Basingstoke Canal: Completed in 1794 the canal is 37 miles long and was originally planned as a major commercial route to link London and Guildford with Southampton via Andover or Winchester. However, the canal's fortunes were never particularly good, its history always somewhat chequered and eventually the western end was filled in, the age of the railway being the final death knell.

In its day the canal carried vessels loaded with coal, grain, malt, timber for ship and house building, chalk and farm produce, among other materials and commodities. Wayward youths, pickpockets and a variety of other criminals often took a ducking in the canal as punishment for their misdeeds.

Restoration work on the canal began in 1973 and much of it was carried out by volunteers, members of the Surrey and Hampshire Canal Society. Reopened by the Duke of Kent in May 1991, much of the Basingstoke Canal is once again navigable and is operated as a leisure project jointly by the Surrey and Hampshire County Councils. There are boats for hire and the canal is stocked with fish including carp and perch. It is, if you like, a linear park with strong emphasis on wildlife and plantlife and the natural environment.

The Waterwitch: Formerly The Cricketers Inn, this public house was renamed The Waterwitch after a narrowboat which used to ply the waters of the canal. The change of name sums up perfectly the council's efforts to restore the Basingstoke Canal to a living waterway.

Odiham Castle was built in 1212 and it was from here that King John, after whom the castle is still sometimes known, set out for Runnymede during the summer of 1215 in order to sign the Magna Carta. In 1216 the castle managed to hold out for two weeks against an attack by a French expeditionary force under the Dauphin. King David of Scotland was held captive in the castle for ten long years in the 14th century. The sole remaining part of the castle today is its intriguing octagonal shaped keep — the only one of its kind in the country.

Greywell Tunnel was built about 1792 and was intended as a short cut to save the Basingstoke Canal a winding 6 mile trip acoss country. The tunnel, at an overall distance of 1,230 yards (nearly a mile), became one of the longest in the south of England. It collapsed in 1872 immediately after a very fortunate bargee had passed through it. The damage was repaired but it collapsed again, 60 years later, in 1932. Like many other canal tunnels it had no towpath and so bargees were forced to 'leg it' — a slow and laborious process which involved using their legs against the walls of the cold dark passage in order to manoeuvre themselves through it.

All Saints church, Odiham: The largest church in North Hampshire was originally Norman though it has become predominantly 14th century. The impressive pulpit carved with scrolls and vases of flowers is worthy of note. The church also includes a 17th century gallery staircase, a 13th century chalk font and the 17th century brick tower. Not far from the north side of the churchyard are stocks together with a whipping post. Inside the churchyard are the graves of several French prisoners from the Napoleonic wars. Nearby is a 'Pest House' into which were incarcerated suspected sufferers from the plague. It is recognisable from its large chimney. Close by also are some almshouses which date from 1623.